BRUNEL

POCKET
GIANTS

D1634535

BRUNEL

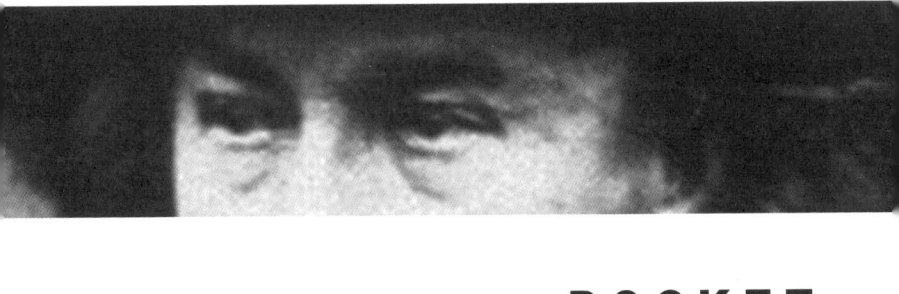

POCKET
GIANTS

EUGENE
BYRNE

The
History
Press

Acknowledgements

Thanks are due to lots of people, but especially Lauren, Monique (but not Jamie), Andrew and Melanie Kelly, Brunel's SS *Great Britain*, Adrian Andrews and the Brunel Institute.

Cover image © Mary Evans Picture Libraray

First published 2014

The History Press
The Mill, Brimscombe Port
Stroud, Gloucestershire, GL5 2QG
www.thehistorypress.co.uk

© Eugene Byrne, 2014

The right of Eugene Byrne to be identified as the Author
of this work has been asserted in accordance with the
Copyright, Designs and Patents Act 1988.

British Library Cataloguing in Publication Data.
A catalogue record for this book is available from the British Library.

ISBN 978 0 7524 9766 2

Typesetting and origination by The History Press
Printed in Europe

Contents

Map

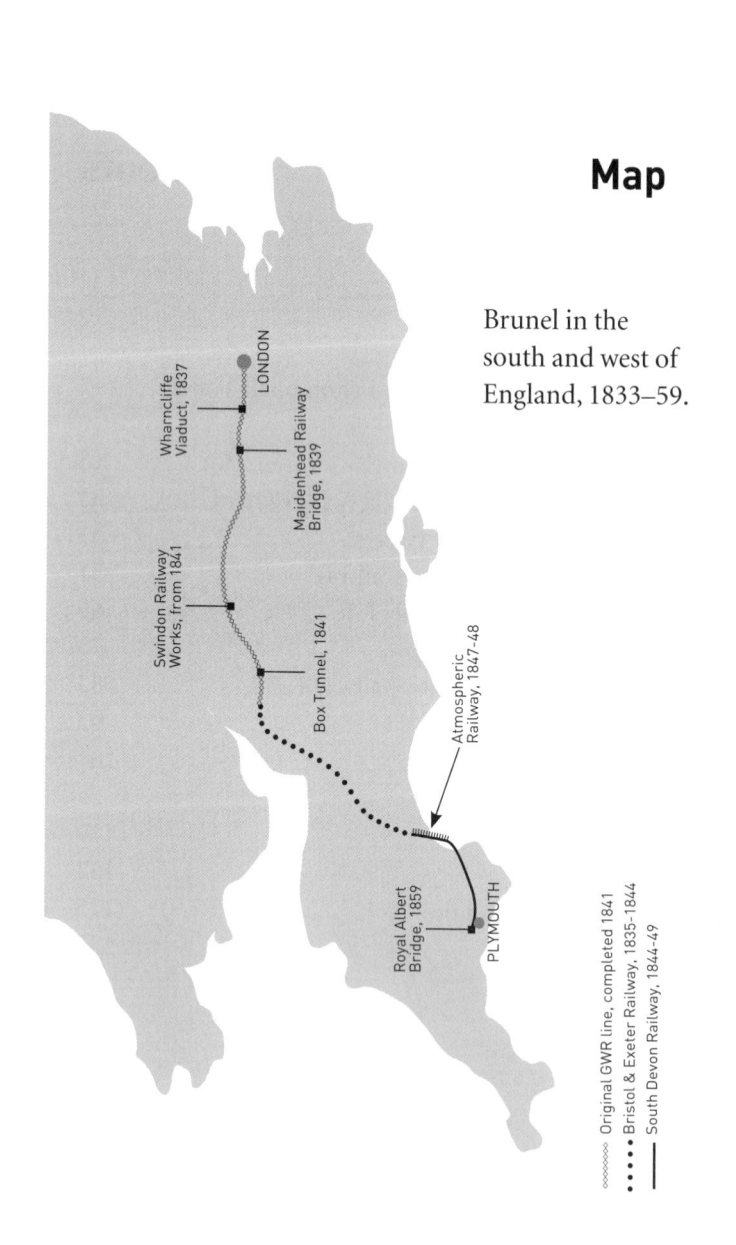

Brunel in the south and west of England, 1833–59.

LONDON

Wharncliffe Viaduct, 1837

Maidenhead Railway Bridge, 1839

Swindon Railway Works, from 1841

Box Tunnel, 1841

Atmospheric Railway, 1847–48

Royal Albert Bridge, 1859

PLYMOUTH

〰〰 Original GWR line, completed 1841
•••• Bristol & Exeter Railway, 1835–1844
—— South Devon Railway, 1844–49

The Second-Greatest Briton of all Time?

'Brunel built the world.'

Isambard Kingdom Brunel was born in Portsmouth and lived in London almost all his life. Yet it is Bristol, a city where he never had any permanent residence, which jealously regards him as its own. Brunel gave the city its trademark Clifton Suspension Bridge and built its peerless rail link to London. In Bristol's harbour, his mighty iron steamship, SS *Great Britain*, arguably the forerunner of all modern ships, is a leading heritage attraction.

It was not always like this. Many of his Bristolian contemporaries took a rather dim view of him. To John Latimer, Bristol's great Victorian journalist and historian, Brunel was 'an inexperienced theorist, enamoured of novelty, prone to seek for difficulties rather than to evade them, and utterly indifferent as to the outlay which his recklessness entailed upon his employers'.[1] Too often, said Latimer, Brunel was allowed to 'indulge his passion for experiments and novelties'[2] when what was needed was hard-headed common sense. Brunel, he went on, had done nothing to prevent Bristol's relative commercial decline as a port, and may even have hastened it. When a new railway station was built at Temple Meads, it was to replace Brunel's original building, which was widely derided by Bristolians.

In 1930, a painting by Ernest Board entitled *Some Who Have Made Bristol Famous* was presented to Bristol's museum and art gallery. This is a fanciful group portrait of figures from different eras in the city's past. It requires an expert knowledge to name even a few of the thirty-nine local worthies in this immense daub, and hardly any will be known to a visitor from elsewhere. Several members of the Wills tobacco dynasty merit inclusion, but of Brunel there is no trace. By 1930 he had been written out of Bristol's history and, by and large, out of the nation's too.

It is very different nowadays. The opening ceremony of the 2012 London Olympics featured Sir Kenneth Branagh as Brunel, choreographing and conducting the Industrial Revolution. Brunel, we were given to understand, was not just a key figure in British history, but one of Britain's greatest gifts to the world.

Brunel's rehabilitation took many years, but had been complete ten years or more before the Olympiad. In a series of programmes in 2002, the BBC asked the public to vote on who they thought were the greatest Britons of all time, with a succession of celebrities, historians and media pundits advocating their own favourites. The case for Brunel was made forcefully by *Top Gear* presenter Jeremy Clarkson: 'Brunel built modern Britain and Britain built the world, which means Brunel built the world.'[3]

In the national poll, Brunel came second, to Winston Churchill, with 350,000 votes.

Brunel had always been known to railway buffs and to aficionados of the heroic Victorian era of British engineering. Indeed, by the 1960s there was a whole university with a strong bias towards technology and engineering named after him. In the consciousness of the wider public, however, he has gone from historical footnote to national icon.

Until recent decades, British schoolchildren were taught that George Stephenson and Richard Trevithick were the real inventors of steam railways. And these men were joined by several others in the pantheon of heroes of the Industrial Revolution. Brunel, if he was mentioned at all, was used as an example of the scale on which Victorians dared to think, usually in the context of his gargantuan ship *Great Eastern*.

In his own time, and for long after, Brunel was a divisive figure. He remained in relative obscurity after his death partly because many of his contemporaries could not see past his costly failures to recognise his lasting achievements. It was not until 1957, when Lionel Rolt, one of the greatest historians of Britain's Industrial Revolution, produced a compelling and entertaining life of Brunel that people started to take notice of him once more. More than fifty years on, and despite the efforts of some historians to take a more balanced and sceptical view, the nation is now madly in love with him.

The main reason for this is that he is media friendly. Brunel's is a colourful story, and it makes for good television. There is the iconic photograph of Brunel, hands in pockets, cigar in mouth and mud on his trousers, taken by photographer Robert Howlett in 1857 at the Millwall dockyards where *Great Eastern* was being built. There are numerous memorial plaques and statues – in Bristol, London (at Temple Meads and Paddington stations), Brunel University, Saltash and Portsmouth, while one at Neyland in Pembrokeshire was stolen in 2010.

Many of the statues have him wearing *that* hat. Brunel always wore the silk hat, even when travelling in his carriage. He claimed that it was both warm and airy at the same time, and that it would afford his head some protection in the event of any objects falling on him. The suspicion must also remain that, at 5ft 4in, he also wore it because it made him look taller.

Then there are the yarns; the cold facts of Brunel's career are remarkable in themselves, but there are numerous legends too. Some are true or half true, but many are complete fictions which nonetheless illustrate some broader point about the man. Here is a good one:

> He once insisted on building a bridge on a principle which was condemned by competent critics. The bridge, which had cost ten thousand pounds, collapsed and the directors remonstrated with their engineer on the waste of money involved. Brunel was equal to the occasion. He triumphantly retorted that he had saved the company hundreds of thousands of pounds, for he argued if the structure had not collapsed he would have built all the bridges on the system the same way.[4]

Brunel's status, then, is not just about the things he built. It's about the whole story of the man, of innovation and of perseverance in the face of adversity and opposition, all leading to great triumphs, and to some equally great disasters. The backstories to most of these projects involve Brunel's brilliance as a showman, a flamboyant and persuasive personality who time and again succeeded in convincing investors to finance his schemes. Then there's the restlessness, the driving ambition which crammed a decade of work, adventure and danger into every year – not forgetting all the accidents and near misses he had as a result of his astonishing physical courage.

But as every scriptwriter and novelist knows, you have to make your good guys a little bit bad – and Brunel had plenty of bad. He was what would now be described as a 'control freak' who found it hard to delegate even small tasks. His supreme self-confidence was actually quite brittle; it could spill over into arrogance and a fear of being challenged by others whose abilities came close to his own. He bullied his staff and contractors and he toadied to authority when his schemes called for it. Throw all the bad into the mix with the good, see how his flaws contributed to his achievements, and there you have your script.

Those who had lost large sums of money on his various projects were possibly not best placed to judge him. From the distance of hindsight, we are in a far better position to evaluate him. Brunel built several structures that are with us to this day, and which still have the power to seduce us with their elegance, their size and how good they look in their settings. Amidst the soaring ambitions of the Victorian age, no engineer thought on a bigger scale than Brunel, and few paid more attention to the quality of what they were building. That he also made ruinously expensive mistakes simply adds to the legend.

Brunel's style, his sheer charisma and the ambition of the things he made speak to us of a type of hero we don't have any more. While there are a handful of, say, architects, who are global celebrities, they are famous simply for being architects. The big engineering projects of today are built by faceless consortia of companies with teams of project managers, architects, financiers, consultants, engineers, lawyers and PR people. Brunel performed most of these roles himself – Lionel Rolt called him the last of Europe's Renaissance men. Brunel was an individualist who dazzled people in his own lifetime and continues to do so today.

What really confers 'giant' status on Brunel is the fact that his greatest works were at the cutting edge of technical possibility. He was not primarily an inventor, but again and again he took the newest technologies and ideas, not just to build bigger or faster, but to do things that more mundane intellects said simply could not be done. Commercial failures at the time were almost always technical triumphs that future generations used and built on.

In his television series *Civilisation*, art historian Kenneth Clark put it best. Brunel, he said, was a born romantic: 'Although the son of a distinguished engineer, brought up in a business that depended on sound calculations, he remained, all his life in love with the impossible.'[5]

1

Marc Isambard Brunel

'Come on, Citizen!'

On 17 January 1793, France's revolutionary regime condemned King Louis XVI to death.

That day, a young French naval officer was sitting with his dog in a cafe in Paris. On hearing the news, he spoke a little too loudly about his feelings and found himself in an angry exchange with some republicans. As he stood up to leave, he summoned his dog ironically: 'Come on, Citizen!'

People were being executed in ever greater numbers for alleged or actual crimes against the revolution. The toll extracted by the guillotine – the 'national razor' as they were starting to call it – would soon peak over a ten-month period known as 'The Terror'. Marc Brunel decided to flee the cafe, flee his lodgings in Paris and, eventually, flee the country.

Marc Isambard Brunel was born in Hacqueville in Normandy in 1769. His family were prosperous farmers, and he was proud of his roots. In a courtroom in England he was once asked if he was a foreigner. 'Yes,' he replied. 'I am a Norman, and it is from Normandy that your oldest nobility derive their titles.'[6]

Isambard was a very uncommon name. It is thought to have derived from the German surname 'Eisenbarth', which may originally have meant 'iron beard' or 'shining iron', which seems appropriate. It may have arrived among the Brunel family of Normandy via some Flemish variation like 'Ysenbaert'.

Marc had an elder brother who would in due course inherit the family landholdings and, as was often the way with second sons of such families, Marc was therefore destined to enter the Church. But by the time he had completed his elementary education it was clear that his talents lay in other areas: his aptitude was for drawing and mechanics. The college principal decided that the boy had no religious calling and helped him transfer to study under François Carpentier, a retired sea captain, for training in hydrography and draughtsmanship. Carpentier was married to one of Marc's cousins and, although French, was also the American consul in Rouen.

At 17 Marc Brunel became a junior officer in the French navy. He served for six years, mostly in the West Indies, aboard the corvette *Le Maréchal de Castries*. By the time he returned, France was in revolutionary ferment. The old order – the *Ancien Régime* – had been overthrown, or so it seemed, and Marc, in that Parisian cafe, was on the wrong side of the new order. He made his way from Paris to his parents' home in Hacqueville. From there he went to Rouen and the house of his mentor, Monsieur Carpentier.

There he met Sophia Kingdom, an English girl about 17 years old. She was the youngest of sixteen children of William Kingdom, a contracting agent for the British army and the Royal Navy. He had died when she was 8 years old, but the family was reasonably well off, and in due course, despite the revolutionary turmoil, she was sent to France to complete her education and improve her French. She also taught English to the children of the local middle classes.

While M. Carpentier was obtaining a passport for Marc to leave for America, the youngsters fell in love. Before he sailed for New York in July 1793, Marc promised he would one day return to her and that they would be married.

Brunel soon found work in America. Working with two other Frenchmen, he carried out a land survey around Lake Ontario. He went on to survey the line of a canal that would eventually link Lake Champlain with the Hudson River. He also submitted a design for a new congress building in Washington; his scheme, modelled on Paris' *Halle aux Grains*, won, though it was never built as it was considered too expensive. A modified version was built as the Park Theatre in New York, but was destroyed by fire in 1821.

Marc gave up his earlier hopes of one day being able to re-join the French navy, and at the age of 27 was appointed chief engineer of New York. But for all America's vast potential, the place for an ambitious engineer was back across the Atlantic. Britain was the seat of the Industrial Revolution, the place where the most exciting new engineering and technology developments were taking place. It was also the home of the largest employer in Europe, an organisation of immense scale and complexity working at the cutting edge of technology: the Royal Navy.

Marc had an idea which he thought would be of use to the navy, and so he set sail for England with a letter of introduction to the First Lord of the Admiralty from a British diplomat in Washington. Equally prominent in his mind – perhaps more so – was the promise he had made to Sophia.

She, meanwhile, had endured adventures of her own. She had remained in Rouen when Marc left for America and had been arrested as an enemy alien when Britain declared war on France in October 1793. She had been taken to the port of Gravelines and incarcerated in a convent which was being used as a temporary prison. A guillotine was set up in the convent courtyard. Some of the families whose children she had taught English intervened to try to secure her release, but to no avail. For almost a year, Sophia lived in daily fear of being executed.

Political changes in Paris finally resulted in the Gravelines prisoners being freed. Sophia, however, was in poor health by this time and it was several months before she was well enough to return to England in 1795.

Marc's ship docked at Falmouth on 7 March 1799. He immediately made for London where Sophia was now living with her brother. Not long afterwards the pair announced their engagement, and they were married at the church of St Andrew in Holborn on 1 November 1799.

'The career of Brunel,' wrote Samuel Smiles, 'was of a more romantic character than falls to the ordinary lot of mechanical engineers.'[7]

Smiles, chronicler of Britain's Industrial Revolution and dour advocate of hard work, common sense and thrift, did not altogether approve of romance, but he did not exaggerate. Marc and Sophia Brunel's courtship, separation and happy reunion was just the beginning of a long and loyal partnership. Marc's career and finances would go through a dramatic sequence of highs and lows, but the couple saw it through together. Indeed, Sophia's devotion to her husband would one day see her in prison for a second time.

The idea Marc brought to England was for a system that could revolutionise industrial production. The Royal Navy needed around 100,000 new pulley blocks every year for raising and lowering the masts and sails on its ships. A single big ship-of-the-line such as Nelson's *Victory* would need well over a thousand blocks on its own.

These blocks were produced by hand, a laborious and expensive process which required skilled workers and often resulted in many blocks being rejected. Marc's invention was intended to change all this via automation. He designed an integrated set of machines, each of which would carry out one small part of the production process.

He had first started thinking about using machines to make the blocks in America. Part of the inspiration came to him when sitting under a tree one day, idly carving letters into its bark and noticing the way in which he was turning his knife: 'And what do you think were the letters I was cutting?' he later wrote. 'Of course none other than S.K.'[8]

On arrival in Britain he lost little time in using his letter of introduction to Earl Spencer, the head of the navy. After some initial setbacks he secured support for his idea from Sir Samuel Bentham, the Inspector General of Naval Works and a distinguished engineer in his own right. (He was also the philosopher Jeremy Bentham's younger brother.)

Marc engaged Henry Maudslay to make the machines. Maudslay was one of the giants of the Industrial Revolution, a tool- and die-maker who is considered by many to be the father of modern machine tool-making. With Bentham's backing, His Majesty's Government approved Marc's proposals in 1803 and within three years he and Maudslay had set up a complete production line at Portsmouth dockyard, where forty-three machines operated by fewer than a dozen unskilled workers did the jobs of sixty craftsmen. The cost saving was reckoned at £24,000 per annum, and for years afterwards distinguished visitors and royal guests came to look in wonder at the machines.

Marc and Sophia had by now moved to Portsmouth to be near the block mills. They already had two daughters, Sophia and Emma. Their only son, Isambard Kingdom Brunel, was born at their home in Britain Street, Portsea, on 9 April 1806.

2

Marc Brunel's Greatest Achievement

'He is a good little boy but he doesn't care for books except mathematics.'

Brunel bequeathed a huge amount of paper to posterity – plans, drawings, letters, notebooks and sketchbooks. As well as these, many of his contemporaries left behind paper trails of their own, or biographies and autobiographies which mention their dealings with him. The only real pity is that Brunel's own attempts at keeping a diary as a young man were so fitful and were eventually abandoned. Much of this material is housed at the Brunel Institute, located next to SS *Great Britain* in Bristol. A fascinating find from recent years is a drawing of his rocking horse. It is almost professional in its quality, yet it was made by a 6-year-old.

Isambard Kingdom Brunel, it is often said, was Marc Brunel's greatest achievement. But his skills were no mere genetic inheritance or the result of ideas casually picked up at the family dinner table. Marc set out in a systematic way to ensure that his only son would be trained, instructed and nurtured as an engineer from an early age.

There were no schools or colleges in Britain from which one could emerge as a qualified civil engineer, so Marc's programme was detailed and thoughtful. The twin starting points of his profession – 'the engineer's alphabet', he called them – were mathematics and drawing. From the age of about 4, Isambard was taught the basics by his father.

The details of Isambard's childhood are obscure. Our only sources are the biography his son wrote and a handful of surviving letters, but it is plain that he was born into a happy and loving family. There are a few glimpses of Isambard as a child. After the family moved to London in 1808, to an address in what is now Cheyne Row, we learn that Isambard learned to swim in the Thames, at the bottom of the garden. Since at this time the river was an open sewer for London's growing population, we might count this as the first of his numerous fortuitous escapes from death.

Around this time, Marc's business began to fluctuate wildly. He had moved his family to London because of his involvement in designing woodworking machines for the government and he also owned a sawmill in Battersea. With the Napoleonic Wars at their height, he had invested in machinery for making boots for the army. He employed disabled ex-soldiers and turned out better and cheaper boots than other contractors. When peace finally returned in 1814, however, he was left with large amounts of unwanted stock. He managed to recoup some of his losses when Napoleon escaped from exile and fighting recommenced, only to see business fall away again after the Battle of Waterloo in June 1815. A few months earlier the sawmill had been destroyed by fire and it was then that Marc found he had been swindled by a business partner. Instead of having £10,000 in the bank, he had just £865.

This was the backdrop as 8-year-old Isambard was sent to Dr Morell's school in Hove. It was an interesting choice, especially if one wishes to class Marc as a social conservative due to his support for the French monarchy. Dr Morell's was probably the most progressive school in the country.

The curriculum included modern languages and geography, as well as the usual Greek and Latin. Bullying was not tolerated and there was no corporal punishment. Neither did the school operate the notorious system of 'fagging' whereby younger boys acted as servants to the older ones. The formal religious dogma of the Anglican Church was not taught either; Dr Morell was a Unitarian minister, and the religious element of the school's curriculum was slight by the standards of the day. Unitarianism was the nearest thing a Victorian could get to agnosticism while still remaining respectable.

Isambard was, if anything, too happy there; halfway through his time at Dr Morell's his father sent him to stay with a relative in France, apparently to straighten him out. 'I entrust my little boy to you as he needs a Mentor,' Marc wrote. 'I don't believe I could make a better choice than in imploring you to moderate the impetuosity of his youth. He is a good little boy but he doesn't care for books except mathematics for which he has a liking.'[9]

Evidently this dose of French discipline worked. By the age of 13, Isambard was writing to his mother to the effect that he liked Horace a lot, but Virgil even more. He also reported that he had been making model boats and that he was amusing himself by making a plan of Hove:

I should be much obliged if you would ask Papa (I hope he is well and hearty) whether he would lend me his long measure. It is a long eighty-foot tape; he will know what I mean. I will take care of it, for I want to take a more exact plan, though this is pretty exact, I think. I have also been drawing a little. I intend to take a view of all (about five) the principal houses in that great town, Hove. I have already taken one or two.[10]

Making drawings and plans of buildings was one of his great boyhood hobbies. According to another possibly apocryphal story, he noticed some new houses being built across the road from his school. He pondered the bad workmanship and, noting the way that the sky promised storms, told his classmates that the buildings would fall down before morning. They found this impossible to believe, so bets were laid, the buildings collapsed overnight and Isambard duly collected his winnings.

In 1820, Marc sent his son to Normandy to study at Caen College. If Britain had the greatest engineers and industrialists at this time, it was widely acknowledged that France had better theoreticians, and Marc believed that this was where his son would find the best education in advanced mathematics. He was also keen that Isambard should improve his French.

From Caen College the boy went on to the Lycée Henri-Quatre in Paris to prepare for the entrance exams for the École Polytechnique, which trained all of France's civil and military engineers. He was turned down, however, as he was not a French national. Instead, Marc secured for his son a period of apprenticeship with Abraham-Louis Bréguet, the world's leading maker of clocks, chronometers and precision instruments. Isambard lived with the Bréguet family in Paris, making plans and drawings of buildings in his spare time and sending them to his father. He would later say that the only qualification in which he took real pride was that he could call himself one of Bréguet's pupils.

While Isambard was with Bréguet, his father and mother were in prison. Marc's money problems had become insuperable. His bankers failed, he was out of credit and he was imprisoned for debt. Sophia insisted on joining him in the King's Bench Prison, Southwark, where they spent ten weeks. One visitor reported that Marc sat at a table working on plans and drawings, while Sophia sat in a corner of the room, mending his stockings.

Marc was angry that he had ended up disgraced through no real fault of his own. The country he had done so much to help in wartime was not showing enough gratitude, he felt, particularly over his losses manufacturing army boots. Letters to influential friends produced no results, so he raised the stakes dramatically. One of the distinguished visitors to the Portsmouth block mills, Tsar Alexander I, had tried to lure him to work in Russia. Marc now let it be known that he was in touch with the Russian government.

The Duke of Wellington, soon to be prime minister, was alarmed at the prospect of Britain losing Marc's talents to the Russians. Now that France had been defeated, Russia was seen as the greatest threat to British interests, both in the Mediterranean and on the north-west frontier of British India. Wellington probably did not know Marc personally, but he would certainly have been aware of his reputation and of how his troops at Waterloo wore Marc's factory's boots. At the Admiralty, Lord Spencer also lobbied for something to be done. The treasury reluctantly paid Marc a grant of £5,000 and the Brunels were freed.

There are interesting parallels between the lives of Brunel, arguably nineteenth-century Britain's greatest engineer, and Charles Dickens, arguably nineteenth-century Britain's greatest novelist. Both men were born in Portsea, within a few streets of each other, and both of their fathers were imprisoned for debt. Both grew up with a powerful work ethic and died relatively young. For Dickens the shame that the debtors' prison brought on the family remained raw and vivid all his life. He drew on the experience of his parents and younger siblings in the Marshalsea Prison for his novel *Little Dorrit.* The effect it had on Isambard is less clear. Living in France through this episode would have insulated him from the excruciating social embarrassment that his mother and sisters must have felt, but it remained seared into the family's collective memory. They referred to it as 'the misfortune', and it is tempting to see anxiety over money and status as one of the drivers of the adult Brunel's commitment to work.

The following year, 1822, Isambard returned from France, now completely fluent. The family was poor, but at least it was out of debt, and his father had plenty of work. He was 16 years old and his formal education was over.

3

Isambard's early career

'My first child, my darling.'

The principal difference between Marc and Isambard Brunel is that Marc invented things, while Isambard adopted and improved existing ideas. Isambard's real apprenticeship now began, working with his father. The breadth of engineering experience he gained at this time was to serve him well in his later career.

The range of projects in which Marc was involved during these years is impressive. He devised a new rotary printing press, a copying machine and a system for making decorative packaging with tinfoil. He already had his sawmill in London; Isambard assisted him in designing another for Trinidad. The end of the Napoleonic conflict opened up business opportunities across the globe beyond the British Empire. Father and son together designed paddle steamers to work on the Rhine and a mill for boring cannon for the Dutch government. Perhaps the most interesting contract of all was from the French government, now restored to the Bourbon monarchy. This was for two suspension bridges for France's Indian Ocean colony, the Île de Bourbon (nowadays La Réunion).

For many years the Brunels also worked on a revolutionary idea which they must have felt could earn a fortune. The concept of the 'gaz engine' was prompted by the work of pioneering scientists Michael Faraday and Humphry Davy. (Now that he was living in London, Marc was mixing freely and on equal terms with the greatest of the capital's scientific minds.) Faraday had been experimenting with using pressure to liquefy various gases, including carbon dioxide. Davy suggested that, since a small amount of heat was needed to change it from liquid back to gas again, the principle could be used as the basis for a new type of engine, potentially cheaper and cleaner than steam.

Marc became fascinated by the idea and he and his son devoted several years – and an estimated £15,000 – to making the concept a practical reality. A patent filed in 1825 describes five cylinders; the outer two contain CO_2 and transfer changes in pressure via two oil-filled cylinders to the one in the middle, which contains a piston. Marc eventually handed over responsibility for the whole project to Isambard, but he was unable, in the end, to make the gaz engine work. The technology did not exist to make joints and casings that could cope with pressures of up to a thousand pounds per square inch without either leaking or exploding.

Isambard struck an introspective note in his diary for October 1827. He was painfully self-conscious:

My self-conceit and love of glory, or rather approbation, vie with each other … The latter is so strong that even of a dark night riding home when I pass some unknown person, who perhaps does not even look at me I catch myself trying to look big on my little pony. I often do the most silly useless things to appear to advantage before, or attract the attention of, those I shall never again see or whom I care nothing about. The former renders me domineering, intolerant, nay even quarrelsome with those who do not flatter me in this case; both combine to make me unpleasant at home.

He was just out of his teenage years, but the insecurity, the admission of a short temper with his family, sound like just about every adolescent boy. Continuing, he went off on a flight of fancy. He often did; he called these fanciful ambitions '*châteaux d'Espagne*' – castles in Spain. Again, he was typically adolescent in his dreams of glory, and not just money:

My ambition, or whatever it may be called (it is not the mere wish to be rich), is rather extensive: but still I am not afraid that I shall be unhappy if I do not reach the rank of hero and Commander in Chief of his Majesty's forces in the gas boat department. This is rather a favourite castle in the air of mine. Make the gaz engine answer, fit out some vessels (of course a war) take some prizes, nay some island or fortified town, get employed by government, construct and command a fine fleet of them and fight;- in fact take Algiers or something in that style. Build a splendid Manufactory for gaz engines, a yard for building the boats for … At last be rich, have a house built of which I have even made the drawings.

At the end he added a giant ambition: 'Be the first Engineer and an example for future ones.'[11]

As he was writing this, Isambard had taken on the first major responsibilities of his career, supervising his father's most ambitious project.

Some years previously, Marc had patented an iron 'tunnelling shield', an idea inspired by the action of *teredo navalis*, the shipworm, which had been a major pest for centuries. The worm (actually a mollusc) has a hard shell at its head which grinds the wood as it moves. It digests the material, which is then secreted as a chalky substance to line the hole it has made behind it.

The shield had now been built and was being used to construct a tunnel under the Thames – the first of its kind. The tunnelling shield worked like a giant shipworm. Miners would work in a series of compartments inside the shield, digging away sections of soil, while bricklayers lined, sealed and secured the tunnel closely behind them. When all the earth within reach of the shield's timbers had been dug out, the whole thing could be moved forward and the process started again.

The Thames Tunnel Company was formed in 1824 to undertake this work, which was urgently needed given the explosive growth in London's population and commerce. The city was divided by the river and desperately needed more ways for people and goods to move across it.

Building more bridges was ruled out as these would be an obstacle to shipping.

Work started in March 1825 near the church of St Mary's Rotherhithe in south-east London. A shaft was dug and an immense brick cylinder 42ft high and 50ft across was built. As the brickwork was finished, workmen dug away the earth beneath and inside it. This allowed the cylinder to sink slowly until its top was flush with ground level. The shield, much of it manufactured by Maudslay, was then lowered down into the chamber and the painstaking work of clearing and backfilling could begin.

It had been assumed that the miners would be digging through clay, but this soon proved a mistake. The shield came up against sand, gravel and rotting sewage. The tunnel was poorly ventilated and the foul-smelling air carried quantities of methane. The men suffered fevers, temporary blindness, vomiting and hallucinations.

The engineer in charge of day-to-day operations, William Armstrong, resigned. Eager to prove himself, 20-year-old Isambard took Armstrong's place and spent days at a time underground, snatching only occasional hours of sleep. Marc became so concerned that he appointed three assistants to help his son. One permanently lost the sight in his left eye, while another died of a fever. Despite all this, and the danger that the Thames, just a few feet overhead, could burst through at any time, the public eagerly queued to pay a shilling to visit the tunnel and witness this unique engineering project. The tunnel company's directors saw this as a way of raising desperately needed revenue.

The first flood happened on 18 May 1827. The water crashed through the ceiling of the tunnel and a huge wave rushed in. Fortunately, the workers had time to run to the shaft and up the steps to the surface and no lives were lost. Isambard rescued one of the older men as he struggled to escape the water.

Undaunted by this mishap, Isambard was out the following day, inspecting the damage from above, using a diving bell. The hole was covered in iron rods, then with bags of clay. Later, he examined the damage inside the tunnel, taking a boat and then crawling along the bank of earth the water had washed in. It took months to clear this debris and pump out the tunnel for work to get under way once more.

In November 1827 Isambard staged a daring publicity stunt to reassure investors and the public that the tunnel was still in business. A banquet was held in the tunnel itself; fifty company directors and other distinguished guests dined, accompanied by music from the band of the Coldstream Guards. At the same time, in another section of the tunnel, some 120 workers sat down to roast beef and beer. They clearly held their boss in high esteem, presenting him with a pick and a shovel as souvenirs.

History does not appear to record how – or if – the filth and stench of the tunnel workings were covered up, but there do not seem to have been any complaints.

This is a particularly good example of the flair for showmanship that Isambard would repeatedly display throughout his career. He even commissioned an artist to record the event. And because it was all Isambard's work, Marc spent the evening at home so that his son could take all the credit and be the centre of attention.

Work on the tunnel started again. Everyone knew that the danger was now at its greatest. Men working at the shield began to dig out old boots, buckles, clay pipes, broken glass and even live eels – sure signs that the riverbed was only just above their heads.

Isambard was at the shield early one morning in January 1828 when the water burst in once more, this time with even greater ferocity than previously. He was swept from the shield and trapped under a fallen timber, suffering a damaged knee and internal injuries which might well have killed an older man. Six others died that day.

Marc took control of the project while his son was recovering, but confidence in the project had collapsed and for some time he was unable to persuade the company's directors to invest further. Work finally resumed in 1835 and the tunnel opened to pedestrians on 25 March 1843 – some eighteen years after work had first commenced. Over 50,000 people walked through it on the first day alone and, as the first tunnel ever to have been built under a navigable river, it was hailed as a modern wonder of the world. It was converted to carry the East London Railway in 1869 and is nowadays part of the London Underground system.

Marc received a knighthood on the personal recommendation of Prince Albert himself – an honour his son never achieved. The project had, however, provided Isambard with a thorough grounding in the day-to-day management of a major undertaking with a large workforce. He had also proved beyond doubt his considerable skills in leadership and public relations, as well as his great physical courage.

It took Isambard a long time to recover fully from the injuries he had sustained in the tunnel collapse. The Brunels' connections with London's scientific elite saw him spending much of 1828 and 1829 working with Michael Faraday, pioneer in the field of electromagnetism, and the inventor Charles Babbage, whose famous Difference Engine is usually claimed as the world's first programmable computer. Thanks to this distinguished company and his own evident talent, Isambard was elected a Fellow of the Royal Society in 1830 at the age of just 24. It was a distinction he wore lightly; once his career had taken off he rarely attended society meetings or lectures.

In 1829 a design competition was launched for a new bridge in Bristol. It was an opportunity Isambard seized eagerly.

Bristol had been an important port since the Middle Ages. Its prosperity was founded on seaborne trade and at one point it may have been the second-largest town in England. Unlike most other places, it was not dominated and shaped by landed aristocrats, but by a closed oligarchy of wealthy merchant families. These men could be ruthless in their pursuit of profit; in the seventeenth and eighteenth centuries some had grown fabulously wealthy on the proceeds of slave trading and sugar plantations worked by slave labour in the West Indies.

By the early nineteenth century, however, Bristol was in relative decline. The smokestack businesses of the Industrial Revolution were mostly in the north and midlands. Moreover, the port was losing Atlantic trade to competition from Liverpool. Part of the problem was that the port lay at the heart of Bristol, at the end of the winding and tidal River Avon. Getting ships in and out was hazardous and time consuming, and ships in the docks were grounded at low tide. The city fathers had tried to overcome this problem in the early 1800s by enclosing a vast amount of water in the central area to create a 'floating harbour'. It had been one of the most spectacular engineering achievements of its day.

Bristol was also a centre for mining and manufacturing. Ever since the Middle Ages, shipbuilders there had designed and built powerful ocean-going merchantmen to take on seas (and a tidal harbour) that would have turned many Mediterranean vessels to matchwood. 'Ship-shape and Bristol fashion,' the saying went.

At this time, the city fathers, encumbered by the cost of building the floating harbour, tended to be conservative and careful, but they could still be ambitious on occasion. One vision they embraced wholeheartedly was a plan to build a bridge across the Avon Gorge. The gorge is the most spectacular natural feature in the area, cutting through a 1½-mile-long limestone ridge just to the west of Bristol proper. In Brunel's time it was situated well away from the town and was a great favourite with painters, who could easily enough reach it on foot, yet at the same time feel as though they were in an unspoiled wilderness.

The money to fund such a scheme began with a bequest made many years earlier. William Vick, a wine merchant, had died in 1764, leaving £1,000 to be administered by the Society of Merchant Venturers, the elite local body representing Bristol's business interests. By 1829, the fund had reached £8,000; nowhere near enough for a stone bridge, but sufficient for much of the cost of an iron suspension bridge. The Merchant Venturers decided to proceed and to look to other methods of raising the additional funds required to link the airy and affluent new suburb of Clifton with the countryside on the Somerset side of the gorge.

The most celebrated new bridge at this time was Thomas Telford's Menai Bridge connecting the island of Anglesey to the Welsh mainland. Built between 1819 and 1826, the suspended part of the roadway spanned 577ft. It was opened with a great fanfare and for many years afterwards attracted visitors who simply wanted to see what *The Times* dubbed 'an extraordinary work of art'.

Telford, Scottish born and largely self-educated, was the leading British engineer of his day. Though he was also an architect and constructor of canals, Telford was best known as a road builder; his friend, the Bristol poet Robert Southey, punningly nicknamed him the 'Colossus of Roads'. The Menai Bridge was both the greatest challenge and the greatest achievement in his grand scheme to improve the route from London to Holyhead – and thence to the Irish Sea and beyond.

Suspension bridges had been around for centuries: a simple row of planks hung from ropes is a suspension bridge. Now, thanks to advances in ironworking, it was possible to build large and robust suspension bridges spanning long distances. The engineering principles are straightforward. The bridge deck is hung – suspended – from vertical cables or rods connected to great iron chains which are anchored firmly in the ground at either end. The chains are usually held aloft by towers at either side of the span. It was a technology that Marc and Isambard both understood fluently. They had, after all, already designed suspension bridges for the French colonies.

A committee of influential Bristol citizens was formed under the chairmanship of the mayor, and an Act of Parliament was sought to gain permission for the bridge. The committee invited engineers to send in plans for what was going to be the highest suspension bridge the world had yet seen, and somewhat longer than the Menai Bridge.

Around twenty plans were submitted by leading engineers. Young Brunel also entered, and his design made it to the shortlist of five finalists which the committee now invited Telford to judge.

The 'colossus' rejected them all. Isambard's was, he recorded, 'pretty and ingenious' but Telford reckoned it would collapse in a high wind. Brunel was certain that the whole gorge could be safely spanned by a suspension bridge, but Telford was not. He ruled that none of the other designs were suitable either, so the committee asked Telford to come up with a design of his own. He came back within a few weeks with an utterly bizarre plan. Since (he believed) the distance could not be bridged by a single span, he proposed a suspension bridge supported by two massive towers ornamented in the Gothic style rising from the bottom of the gorge.

Isambard was furious. He sarcastically wrote to the bridge committee:

> As the distance between the opposite rocks was considerably less than what has always been considered as being within the limits to which suspension bridges might be carried, the idea of going to the bottom of the valley for the purpose of raising, at great expense, two intermediate supporters, hardly occurred to me … what a reflection such timidity will cast on the state of the Arts today![12]

Thomas Telford was the elder statesman of British engineering, while Brunel was just a youthful upstart, albeit one with a famous father. The committee was, however, conscious of the costs involved in the Telford scheme and decided to announce a new competition, which would be judged by John Seward, a London iron manufacturer and mathematician, and Davies Gilbert, a Cornish engineer and expert on suspension bridges.

Telford's design was tactfully 'set aside' on grounds of expense. In a meeting with Gilbert, Brunel produced detailed drawings and mathematical calculations. He won the day. Gilbert did, however, require a lot of changes.

Telford's views on the safe length of the span prevailed up to a point. It was to be limited to 703ft. Isambard submitted a new design – with some help from his father – this time with one of the towers held up by a huge brick support on the rocks on the western side. This abutment added £14,000 to the final cost. The plan was for it to be decorated in the then fashionable Egyptian style and for its towers to feature cast-iron reliefs of the processes involved in making the bridge.

The Egyptian theme charmed Bristol and the bridge committee. Isambard wrote to a friend: 'Of all the wonderful feats I have performed since I have been in this part of the world, I think yesterday I performed the most wonderful. I produced unanimity among fifteen men who were all quarrelling about that most ticklish subject – taste.'

He was extremely pleased with himself. 'The Egyptian thing I brought down,' he continued, 'was quite extravagantly admired by all and unanimously adopted: and I am directed to make such drawings, lithographs etc., as I, in my supreme judgement, may deem fit …'[13]

On 21 June 1831, a grand ceremony took place as work started on the bridge. Sir Abraham Elton, an important local landowner and businessman, made a very flattering speech. He could anticipate the time, he said, when:

as the young gentleman who had been selected (young as he was) to conduct this undertaking of such magnitude, would pass from city to city, and the cry would be raised: 'There goes the man who reared that stupendous work, the ornament of Bristol and the wonder of the age.'

A toast to the success of the undertaking was then drunk in sparkling champagne. 'The humbler classes were regaled with a barrel of beer,' reported the *Bristol Mercury*, 'and the ceremony terminated much to the satisfaction of every one.'[14]

Brunel took up occasional residence in Bristol, usually staying at the Bath Hotel – the building does not exist any longer – overlooking the eastern side of the bridge works. But any elation he may have felt that he was finally starting out independently on his career was to be short-lived. The bridge's auspicious beginning would prove to be the first of many false starts on the project he would call 'my first child, my darling'.[15] Work on the bridge was stopped by civil unrest and violence on a massive scale.

The riots that erupted at the end of October 1831 were some of the most serious disturbances Bristol had ever seen. The unrest was mirrored on a smaller scale elsewhere in the country. The issue was parliamentary reform, and demands not just that more people should be allowed the vote but that representation should be fairer. So-called 'rotten boroughs' returned one or two MPs, even though they had little or no population at all, while major new population centres, especially in the midlands and north, had just one MP or none at all. Into this toxic mix went a major economic downturn and rising grain prices which caused great distress among the working classes.

The Bristol riots were sparked after the House of Lords, standing up for the privileges of the old order, rejected the second reform bill. Sir Charles Wetherell, a judge with decidedly anti-reform views, arrived in Bristol and was followed by an angry crowd to Queen Square, home to many of the local elite and site of the Mansion House, the mayor's residence. Over the following days, the mob looted and burned the homes of unpopular figures, and broke open the prisons and set the inmates free.

At first, many middle-class Bristolians watched the discomfiture of the city fathers with amusement. But then things got out of hand and, when a small detachment of soldiers appeared unable to cope, law-abiding folk were enlisted as special constables to try to restore order. Brunel was one of the volunteers. He succeeded in arresting a burly rioter, but the man later escaped when some of his friends, masquerading as constables themselves, relieved Brunel of his charge. In the end, it was ruthless action by the army, rather than the concerned citizens, that brought the riots to an end.

Isambard rarely spoke or wrote about party politics, though decoding his broader ideological outlook is easy. The actions he took and the attitudes he displayed throughout his career place him clearly at the *laissez-faire* end of nineteenth-century liberalism. He was emphatically in favour of free trade, and believed people should be allowed to do business and make things as they pleased (provided they did no harm) without interference from government or bureaucrats. Later in his career he even called for the abolition of patents, so that anyone would be free to adopt and improve new ideas.

His voluntary action during the riots should not be taken to mean that he objected to parliamentary reform. He was simply opposing disorder and mob rule. Indeed, he would serve as a special constable once more in 1848, when the government, fearing revolutionary uprisings like those taking place on the Continent, panicked over the great Chartist meeting in London.

Brunel was a member of the same up-and-coming middle classes who stood to gain most from reform, and his writings hint that he was passionately in favour of it. To reformers, the country's entire system of government was archaic, corrupt, inefficient and biased in favour of rural and aristocratic interests at the expense of industry, enterprise and cities. The year after the Bristol riots, he helped in a successful campaign to elect his close friend and brother-in-law Benjamin Hawes (who had married Brunel's sister Sophia in 1820) as the Whig candidate for Lambeth. By the standards of the time, Hawes was a radical, opposed to the Corn Laws (which set grain prices artificially high to benefit British landowners) and in favour of extending the vote to more people.

The riots dented business confidence in Bristol, and work on the bridge was suspended. It only resumed in August 1836. There was a second foundation ceremony at which Isambard slung an iron pole 1in in diameter across the gorge. From this was suspended a basket which could be moved from one side to the other with pulleys. The bar sagged in the middle and the basket got stuck. Once it was moving again Isambard insisted on being the next to cross. It got stuck once more, and in a characteristic display of bravado, he climbed out of the basket, 300ft up in the air, and freed it, to the delight of thousands of onlookers.

Progress was slow. In 1843 the money ran out and work stopped again. The bare towers became known to Bristolians as 'Vicksville' (after William Vick). The one on the Clifton side became a popular picnic spot. The bar and its travelling basket remained in place for some years. It became a popular white-knuckle ride. In one famous incident a couple who had just got married travelled across. In the words of John Latimer in his *Annals of Bristol in the Nineteenth Century*: 'Unfortunately the hauling ropes got out of order just as they reached the middle of the bar, and they were left for some hours to discuss the beauty of the scenery.'[16] On another occasion, an effigy of an unpopular politician was hung from the bar at election time, and the services of a marksman had to be engaged to break the rope.

The bridge would not be completed in Brunel's lifetime.

4

The Great Western Railway

'Brunel's billiard table.'

In late 1831, while travelling in northern England seeking work from various contacts, Isambard was a passenger on the Liverpool & Manchester Railway. It was his first ever train journey, and he was intrigued. He drew lines and circles in his notebook. 'I record this specimen of the shaking on the Manchester Railway,' he wrote. 'The time is not far off when we shall be able to take our coffee and write whilst going noiselessly and smoothly at 45 mph.'[17]

Steam engines had been in use for over a century, powering mine pumps and factory machines and, increasingly, boats and ships. 'Rail ways' were nothing new either: wagons hauled along rails by horses, ponies or men (and even women and children) were common in Britain's mines. Mining engineers Richard Trevithick (1771–1833) and John Blenkinsop (1783–1831) had both experimented with steam-powered engines hauling colliery wagons, but the real father of railways was George Stephenson (1791–1848).

Like Trevithick and Blenkinsop, Stephenson initially designed steam 'locomotives' to haul wagons along iron rails at collieries. Then he extended his ambitions. On 27 September 1825, the Stockton & Darlington Railway opened, with a steam engine designed and driven by Stephenson. It hauled 80 tons of coal and flour, along with the world's first passenger carriage, for 9 miles, reaching a speed of 24mph. Within five years he had built a line between Liverpool and Manchester.

Britain pioneered railways, which were quickly copied around the world. Unlike many other countries, where infrastructure projects were directed by government, Britain's railways were built by private companies, funded by wealthy and modest investors alike. The result was periods of 'railway mania', speculative bubbles that could burst with spectacular and catastrophic consequences for shareholders.

During his career, Brunel was designer or consultant for numerous rail companies in the British Isles and Europe, but the one with which his name will always be associated is the Great Western Railway (GWR).

Over the winter of 1832/33 a consortium of businessmen in Bristol began to discuss the possibility of building a railway line to London. To them, this was both a business opportunity and a way of hitting back at their great maritime rival, Liverpool. The Corporation, the Docks Company, the Merchant Venturers and the Chamber of Commerce formed a committee to commission a survey of the proposed railway route and then to present a bill to parliament seeking permission for the line. Brunel applied for the position of engineer to carry out the survey.

Until the GWR came along, the quickest way of travelling inland in Britain was by coach. The mail coach was expensive and uncomfortable, but it was reliable and, by the standards of horse-drawn travel, it was fast. The journey from London to Bristol – almost 120 miles – could be covered in sixteen hours and forty-five minutes, stopping regularly at posts (usually inns) along the way to change horses. People set their watches by the almost always punctual mail coach.

On 6 March 1833, Brunel took an overnight coach from London to Bristol, sitting on the outside as it was cheaper. At 2 p.m. the following day he was told that his friends and contacts in Bristol had stood him in good stead. The committee had evidently deliberated a great deal over placing their trust in this young man, but had decided to give him the job by a majority of just one vote. This was on condition that he would be accompanied by an older and experienced Bristol engineer named William Townsend.

Surveying started on 9 March 1833. Townsend came along too, to Brunel's evident irritation. Townsend soon faded from the picture; aware that he was neither wanted nor needed, he contented himself with working for Brunel from an office in Bristol.

There followed a gruelling four months as Brunel travelled on horseback or by coach exploring the land between Bristol and London and deciding the optimal route. He usually spent the night at inns, often sleeping for only a few hours. Some nights he worked so hard on the plans that he hardly slept at all.

Four months later, he presented his survey to the committee in Bristol. The line he proposed would be

116 miles long and would cost, he estimated, £2½ million. Trying to translate this sum into modern values is futile, though it would probably amount to billions.

The company went to London for help with the finance. A committee was set up in the capital and, about this time, the name 'Great Western Railway' first started being used. The origins of the name are disputed. It may have been Brunel's idea. It certainly sounded as grandiose as its ambitions and might have been prompted by Marc's use of the word 'great' for some of his projects. The most likely derivation, though, is surely that this was going to be the rail counterpart to the 'Great West Road' running from Bristol to London (the modern-day A4).

In August 1833, Brunel was formally appointed as engineer for the railway at a salary of £2,000 a year – a sizeable sum for the time, although he also had to fund his office and pay assistants from it. The trust that the directors placed in a largely untried man of 26 says something about Brunel's reputation (and perhaps that of his father); but ultimately he got the job because there were very few other contenders. Brunel was working at the forefront of a completely new and radical technology. Perhaps a useful parallel from recent decades would be the young men and women running the first dot-com companies.

Brunel leased a house at 53 Parliament Street in London and commissioned the building of his own special coach, in which he would be travelling a great deal. It was based on a type of horse-drawn carriage known as a 'britzka'. In it were a drawing board, cupboards for his equipment, a folding bed and sufficient storage for fifty cigars (it is unclear when he picked up the habit, but by now he had been a heavy smoker for some years). The britzka had no windows, so that when travelling he could remain focused on work and not be distracted by the scenery. He was accustomed to moving it around quickly, even recklessly. Railway workers would later nickname it 'The Flying Hearse'.

Brunel's two immediate tasks were to carry out a far more detailed survey of the route and to help secure parliamentary approval. Both issues he attacked with extraordinary energy. St George Burke, a lawyer engaged by the GWR, later recalled working with Brunel. His home was directly opposite, and Brunel ran a piece of string from his own house to a bell in Burke's so that he could summon the lawyer's attention at any time or, if they had to travel on business, wake him up. Burke later wrote: 'It was his frequent practice to rouse me out of bed about three, by means of the bell. I would invariably find him up and dressed and in great glee at the fun of having curtailed my slumbers by two or three hours more than necessary.'[18]

For all the work involved, Brunel was having a splendid time. George Clark, who worked closely with him as one of his assistants during the early days of GWR, later wrote: 'His light and joyous disposition was very attractive. At no time was he stern but when travelling or off work he was like a boy set free. There was no fun for which he was not ready.'[19]

Securing parliamentary consent for the GWR was challenging. The company initially applied for approval for lines from Bristol to Bath and London to Reading, the assumption being that the section in between could be built later when sufficient capital had been secured. Many MPs came under pressure from vested interests. Farmers close to London feared competition from rivals further away who would be able to send their produce to market by rail. Canal and stagecoach owners were concerned that their business would disappear. Maidenhead worried about losing its bridge tolls. Eton School worried that quick and easy travel would carry its young gentlemen to the brothels and gambling hells of London. An apocryphal story had the Duke of Wellington, hero of Waterloo and now prime minister, complaining that railways would 'encourage the lower classes to move about needlessly'. Parliament rejected the bill.

GWR returned the following year, 1835, seeking permission for the entire line, having raised enough money to fund the project in full. As with the first bill, Brunel spent several days being examined by MPs at the committee stage. He remained polite, charming and cool throughout, evidently enjoying himself. Word got around of his performance and people started coming to watch him. One witness later said:

> The committee room was crowded with landowners and others interested in the success or defeat of the Bill, and eager to hear his evidence. His knowledge of the country surveyed by him was marvellously great, and the explanations he gave of his plans, and answers to questions … showed a profound

acquaintance with the principles of mechanics. He was rapid in thought, clear in his language, and never said too much, or lost his presence of mind.[20]

The Great Western Railway Bill was passed on 31 August 1835.

Of all Brunel's achievements, many would argue that the GWR is the greatest. It was the first railway conceived as a complete system. Brunel thought through every aspect of it, from engineering works to locomotives and rolling stock, signalling and buildings. It was also a masterpiece of surveying and gradation; he made the line as flat and as straight as possible. It would come to be nicknamed 'Brunel's Billiard Table'.

The permanent way was a masterpiece in itself, though there were initial problems. The rails rested on sleepers, which turned out to be too firmly fixed to the ground by piles, resulting in an uncomfortable ride for passengers. So the piles were removed to give the rails more flexibility.

The line also included several structures – cuttings, tunnels and bridges – which were all successful in their own terms. One of the first major structures Brunel constructed was the viaduct over the Brent Valley at Hanwell, west London. Built of bricks and still in use to this day, this was one of the first sights that the public beyond Bristol had of his talents as a designer, though, as with the Clifton Suspension Bridge, his father was in the background with advice. In a characteristic flourish of political know-how, Brunel named it the Wharncliffe

Viaduct in honour of Lord Wharncliffe, the influential member of the House of Lords committee that had passed GWR's Act of Parliament.

The bridge over the Thames at Maidenhead was another great achievement; some commentators even claim it as the greatest single structure he ever built. The railway had to cross 300ft of river, though there was a small island in the middle. Here he placed a central pier. Then on either side he built the two widest arches (of brick) that the world had ever seen. These arches had to be extremely shallow, and because of this many experts predicted that they must surely collapse. That was in 1838; but the bridge is still standing to this day and still carrying trains. Aware of growing concerns about its stability and equally certain of his own meticulous calculations, Brunel had a great deal of fun leaving the scaffolding up around the bridge long after it was completed, pretending that he too feared it was about to fall down.

The line was built by contractors, each one responsible for a set length of the track. Thousands of labourers were employed – known as navvies, from 'navigators', the name given the workmen who had dug Britain's canals in previous generations. One of the greatest wonders of the Great Western, as with most other engineering feats of the period, is that it was constructed without machines. Steam engines were sometimes used to pump water from workings and gunpowder was used to break up rock, but the GWR was essentially built by the sweat and muscle of men and horses.

This was not cheap. Cost overruns would be one of the defining characteristics of Brunel's career. In some ways, this is a paradox; for on a day-to-day basis, the records show that he was extremely careful with the company's money. This was especially the case in his relationships with the contractors. He tended to hire the company offering the lowest price and, as was the practice at the time, he demanded a cash bond of up to £5,000, repayable one year after the work had been carried out to the company's – i.e. Brunel's – satisfaction.

Time and again he withheld some or all of this money. Repayment of bonds and other disputes with contractors often ended in the courts and the outcome was not always to GWR's advantage. The worst case was with the partnership of Hugh McIntosh and his son David, who took over the work of a failed contractor on the line. David McIntosh was far superior to the normal line of contractors, who were usually self-made men with hard-won practical experience. McIntosh had plenty of this (and his father had even more), but was also well educated and a highly capable engineer. He and Brunel seem to have taken an instant dislike to one another. McIntosh resented Brunel's overbearing manner and, most Brunel biographers agree, the latter felt threatened by his contractor's undoubted talents. The dispute between Brunel and the McIntoshes was long and complex, but the contractors ended up out of pocket to the tune of £100,000 and decided to sue. The case dragged through the courts for over twenty years and was only settled in

1865, after Brunel had died. David McIntosh – his father had long since died – finally won, a victory that pushed GWR close to bankruptcy.

The McIntoshes should have been valued partners. Capable contractors would ultimately have saved the company a lot of money. But Brunel's choice of the cheapest, together with his haughty manner and financial haggling, put many of the better ones off tendering for work at all, and ended up costing money to put mistakes right. This, along with Brunel's quest for perfection in everything and the fact that he had surely underestimated the cost of the railway in the first place, meant that by the time it was finished, the GWR had cost £6.5 million, well over twice his original estimate.

There was another price as well. Hundreds of working men and boys paid with their health and even their lives. The exact number of accidental deaths and injuries among the thousands who worked on the GWR is unknown. We do, however, know that at least a hundred were killed working on the Box Tunnel, the most ambitious project on the whole line. Those who died, and who mostly went to paupers' graves paid for by their comrades, were little noted by wider society at the time. Brunel himself was largely unconcerned by the casualties; as far as he was concerned, that was the business of contractors and no one else. This was all characteristic of his *laissez-faire* outlook. He was opposed to legislation to regulate wages and working conditions, telling a parliamentary inquiry that such 'interference' would only cause mischief and that it would 'injure the skill, activity and independence of the labourer'.[21] Perhaps the most hypocritical delusion of these nineteenth-century economic liberals was that working men had the same opportunities and freedom to choose as the middle classes. The best one can say for Brunel was that he was a creature of his times, that deaths and injuries are part of the collateral damage of construction projects even to this day and that all he really cared about was getting the job done.

The tunnel was driven through Box Hill, halfway between Bath and Chippenham. At nearly 2 miles, it was the longest railway tunnel in the world at the time. It took five years to dig, consuming a ton of candles and a ton of gunpowder each week. About a quarter of the tunnel at the eastern end runs through solid rock, but the rest of it is through clay and softer rock and so was lined with 30 million bricks.

When the two ends of the tunnel were joined up, there was less than 2in of error in their alignment. Brunel was there when they broke through and was so pleased he pulled a ring from his finger and gave it to the foreman in charge of the navvies.

One of the most famous Brunel legends claims he deliberately aligned the Box Tunnel so that the rising sun would shine straight through it every 9 April – his birthday. Brunel's biographers and other experts have long debated the veracity of this story; the consensus seems to be that it may well be true, but it remains unproven. It would certainly have been a joke entirely in keeping with its creator's character.

5

Marriage and Family Life

'Will it make me happier?'

Brunel drove himself hard, and he expected others to do likewise. His gargantuan self-assurance occasionally spilled over into arrogance and an unwillingness to listen to others more experienced and knowledgeable. He also had a notorious temper which terrorised many of the younger men who came to work for him:

> During the latter part of the professional career of Mr. Brunel … and before failing health and loss of nerve caused him to lose that absolute independence of action which, in his best days, he maintained with reference to the Directors of his various undertakings, it was neither unsafe nor unpleasant thus to execute his orders. Admit him to be absolute and he was not only reasonable, but kind. Hint to him that you had rights, and he was inexorable.[22]

This was in later life, as the burdens of responsibility started to take their toll. It is very illuminating that when Brunel's son wrote to St George Burke seeking recollections of working with his father, the lawyer felt it necessary to explain how Brunel had been a very different man in his younger days:

In the midst of the heaviest and most responsible labours, he could enter into the most boyish pranks and fun, without in the least distracting his attention from the matter of business in which he was engaged; but all who knew him as I did could bear testimony to this characteristic of his disposition. I believe that a more joyous nature, combined·with the highest intellectual faculties, was never created, and I love to think of him in the character of the ever gay and kind-hearted friend of my early years, rather than in the more serious professional aspect under which your pages will, no doubt, rightly depict him.[23]

Brunel was always a gregarious character, but he had relatively few close friendships. Of these, the most interesting is that with Robert Stephenson (1803–59), perhaps because they had so much in common. Both were engineers at the top of their profession, both were the sons of famous engineers (Robert was the son of George Stephenson) and they were of a similar age. They could easily have been bitter professional rivals, but instead tended to support one another. 'Stephenson is the only man in the profession that I feel disposed to meet as my equal, or superior, perhaps,' Brunel wrote. 'He has a truly mechanical head.'[24]

Isambard also seems to have been a hit with the girls, and his journals hint at a few romances. The most important was with Ellen Hume or Hulme, from a family in Manchester who were in some way acquainted with the

Brunels. Brunel's diaries mention a John Hulme, Ellen's brother, though we know little more about the family.

'Devilish pretty,' he wrote, 'but I'm afraid those eyes don't speak of a very placid temper.' Other comments about her in his diary appear to have been cut out.[25]

She seems not to have married, and during the 1840s he appears to have been supporting her and her sister financially. There is nothing to suggest any impropriety or that she was his mistress, but he did arrange to pay her an annuity in later life. Their youthful romance, which may have started when Isambard was as young as 14, might well have turned to marriage in due course, but until his mid-twenties he did not feel financially secure enough to support a wife and family.

By December 1835 everything had changed. He was in charge of building the GWR, and this alone provided a good salary. He was also engineer to several smaller railways as well as various other building projects around the country. His work at Bristol docks had been a great success, and the Clifton bridge would soon be under way once more. His father, meanwhile, had resumed excavation of the Thames Tunnel.

In a moment of introspection he made a list in his fitfully kept journal of all the projects he was involved with. In all, he was responsible for over £5 million worth of work:

I really can hardly believe it when I think of it.

I go sometimes with my four horses – I have a cab and horse – I have a secretary – in fact I am now a somebody. Everything has prospered … I don't like it. It can't last. Bad weather must surely come. Let me see the storm in time to gather in my sails.

This time twelve months I shall be a married man. How will that be? Will it make me happier?[26]

Three years previously he had been introduced by his friend Benjamin Hawes to the Horsley family in Kensington. William Horsley was a distinguished organist and composer; his best-known composition nowadays would probably be the setting for the hymn *There is a Green Hill Far Away*. His wife Elizabeth was the daughter of an organist and composer, and all but one of their five children were talented musicians or artists.

The Horsleys' home was regularly visited by some of the finest musicians in Europe, including Mendelssohn, Brahms and the great violinist Paganini. Brunel spent many happy evenings there. The Horsleys and their guests listened to music, played instruments, and wrote and performed little plays and sketches. It was characteristic of Brunel, with his sense of fun and showmanship, that he entertained them with conjuring tricks.

John Callcott Horsley became a close friend. (He is generally credited with having made the first ever Christmas card, and in later life he campaigned against gratuitous nudity in art and was ridiculed as 'Clothes-Horsley'.) The oldest of William Horsley's three daughters, Mary, was the only one of his children with no obvious artistic talent, but she was regarded as a great beauty. It was to her that Brunel proposed. They married at Kensington parish church on 5 July 1836.

The honeymoon was a two-week tour to North Wales, then on to Devon and back to London. While it included a ride on the Liverpool & Manchester Railway, most of their journeys were by coach.

There seems something rather calculating about Isambard's marriage, although it was entirely conventional by the standards of the time. It seems to have been an entirely happy match, but it was also a business arrangement. Mary Horsley was getting a husband who had a glittering career ahead of him and he was getting one of the most glamorous women in London. She appealed to his sense of taste and style. And there was something grand, possibly even haughty, about her. Her sisters nicknamed her 'The Duchess of Kensington'. It was perhaps rather telling that the Brunels' establishment of servants included a footman, a decorative but otherwise pointless flunkey whose principal role was to attend to his mistress whenever she left the house.

Mary was also an acknowledged leader in fashion. When she was presented to Queen Victoria her niece wrote: 'The Queen never took her eyes off aunt Mary, but followed her to the end of the room, and I had no chance of being noticed, coming behind her immense crinoline.'[27]

They lived at 18 Duke Street, a smart address near St James's Park, which Brunel had acquired shortly before getting married. The house was later extended next door, as his young family grew. His parents, troubled by money problems to the end, also moved in with them. This was not an entirely untroubled arrangement; there are hints at some needle between Sophia and Mary, with Brunel's mother apparently disapproving of the large amounts of her son's money that Mary spent on fashionable living, particularly clothes.

In addition to the footman, there was a butler, a cook and the usual array of other, mostly female, servants. The house was fitted out with the best furniture and fittings money could buy. The walls were hung with paintings by some of the leading artists of the day, including Sir Edwin Landseer and (of course) John Callcott Horsley. An inventory of the house contents made in 1858 values everything at £8,300. This was at a time when a skilled working man might hope to earn about £100 in a year.

The Brunels had three children. Isambard (1837–1902) had a leg disability but went on to become a successful lawyer. Henry Marc (1842–1903) followed his father into the engineering profession. The youngest child was Florence Mary (?1847–76); she married a teacher and was the only Brunel child to have children of her own.

Isambard, Mary and the children were, of course, among the first Britons to take holidays by train, visiting former fishing villages, which the railways were now turning into seaside resorts. On a holiday in Torquay, Brunel was so taken with the area that in the 1840s he bought a plot of land at the town's outskirts on which to build a house, later purchasing 500 acres of surrounding land to extend the estate. He drew up plans for a big house in the Italianate style and planned out the gardens. The building's foundations were laid but he never found the time to finish it. It was sold after his death and a different design erected on the foundations.

From the surviving family letters we can see that, just like Marc, Isambard was a loving father. Victorian fathers were traditionally meant to be authoritarian and rather distant figures, though when Brunel's children were younger we have accounts of how he would eagerly race up the stairs when he got home to see them and to play with them.

The family did not see much of him, however, as time went on. He was often either away or working long hours in his office at home. In fact, Christmas was the only day of the year when he did not work. But there is no doubt that Brunel loved children and, even before his own were born, he was a favourite uncle figure to many friends' and relatives' youngsters. Whenever he could spare the time, he would play with his own children, take them to the zoo or circus and, every Christmas, to the pantomime. He also liked to entertain them with his famous conjuring tricks.

One such trick nearly killed him. On 3 April 1843, he was showing them one of his favourites – pretending to swallow a coin (a gold half-sovereign) and then appearing to take it out of his ear. The coin accidentally slipped down his throat and became lodged in his right bronchus, resulting in periodic violent coughing fits. Several attempts to remove it, including a tracheotomy, failed, and the coughing left him exhausted for days at a time. Finally, at Marc's suggestion, he was strapped to a table that was held upside down while his back was struck gently. The treatment worked. Such was his fame by then that the case was closely followed by the nation's newspapers, even *The Times*.

The distance between Brunel and his children increased as they got older, particularly once the boys were sent away to boarding schools. We have a letter he wrote to Mary about Isambard Jr, whose bad leg would surely have made him a prime victim for bullies, in which he tried to console her by claiming that he had been through the same thing when he was the boy's age. Given the liberal regime of Dr Morrell's in Hove, he was either lying or he genuinely did not know quite how awful most traditional schools were.

Like many Victorians, Brunel actually found it easier to express emotions and feelings in letters rather than in person. He wrote to Isambard on his eighteenth birthday: 'My dear Isambard, although my constant engagements have prevented me seeing so much of my children as I have wished … I hope that you would look on me as your first friend if you ever got into difficulty.'[28]

Brunel's sons plainly had a great deal of respect for their father and, between the lines, affection as well. It was they who produced the first biography of their father (the brothers had refused to collaborate with or authorise any other would-be writers), Isambard Jr doing the writing, supported by Henry who provided extensive notes on technical engineering matters.

6

The First Two Ships

'This huge thing of life.'

In October 1835, at a meeting of the GWR directors in London, Brunel made an offhand remark when someone spoke of the length of the line and its mounting costs: 'Why not make it longer, and have a steamboat go from Bristol to New York?'

Soon it was no longer a joke. After all, it made perfect sense. People wishing to travel to the US could take the GWR from London to Bristol and embark on a steamship that would take them across the Atlantic faster and more reliably than a conventional sailing vessel.

There were already regular passenger 'packet ships' sailing between Britain and the US, but they were slow. Given the vagaries of weather it was impossible to timetable them precisely. Worst of all, crossing the Atlantic in a small wooden sailing ship was not a pleasant experience. Passengers got bored in good weather, seasick in bad and terrified in the worst. It was a journey that all passengers prayed would be over as quickly as possible.

No ship had yet crossed the Atlantic by steam power alone. A prevalent view was that no steamer could carry enough coal for such a long voyage. Marine engineers were, however, beginning to realise that a ship's carrying capacity increases as the cubic multiple of the hull's dimensions, whereas the water resistance only increases as its square.

Brunel is usually depicted as an obsessive, who took charge of every aspect of any project, but for his first ship he deferred to the knowledge of others. The leading lights of the Great Western Steamship Company (a newly established firm, separate from the railway) were Brunel, his friend, Bristol businessman Thomas Guppy, Bristol shipbuilder William Patterson and semi-retired naval officer Christopher Claxton, also a Bristolian.

Patterson and Claxton toured the country investigating steamship technology. A ship that could cross the Atlantic was perfectly feasible, they reported, but it would have to be the largest ever built. They estimated that a steamship displacing 1,200 tons, carrying 580 tons of coal, could cross to the US in less than twenty days going west and return in thirteen – half the time of the average sail voyage.

Patterson designed the ship, while Brunel oversaw her engines, which were built by Maudslay, Son and Field. *Great Western* was launched from Patterson's yard at the Western Wapping Dock in Bristol on 19 July 1837, and made her way under sail to London where her engines were fitted. She performed well in trials on the Thames and on 31 March 1838 set off back for Bristol to pick up passengers for her maiden voyage. Brunel and Claxton were on board and Lieutenant James Hosken, an experienced naval captain, was in charge.

As the mighty ship passed near Canvey Island black smoke began to billow out from around the base of her funnel. Stokers ran up from the engine room in panic and Hosken ran her on to some sandbanks. Brunel rushed below to inspect the damage, not realising that the ladder had been damaged by the fire. A rung broke and he fell, landing on Claxton. He was carried out, seriously injured.

The damage to *Great Western* was less serious. Felt insulation at the base of the funnel had overheated and caught fire but this was easily fixed. She was floated off the sandbanks on the next high tide and Hosken and Claxton took her to the Bristol Channel, where she moored at Broad Pill near Avonmouth and took on coal.

The damage to *Great Western*'s reputation was more severe. News of the fire prompted fifty nervous passengers to cancel their bookings. Nonetheless, hundreds of well-wishers came to see her off as she left for New York on 8 April 1838 under the command of Lt Hosken. Brunel was still recovering from his injuries at home.

The transatlantic passenger business was extremely competitive and the first to cross under steam could anticipate healthy profits. *Great Western* had a rival. The British & American Steam Navigation Co., founded by American lawyer Junius Smith and Scottish shipbuilder Macgregor Laird, were planning a steamer of their own, but construction had not yet started. So they chartered *Sirius*, a small steamer that had been built to travel between Britain and Ireland, and decided to pit her against the world's first purpose-built Atlantic steamer.

Because of *Great Western*'s fire, *Sirius* got a four-day head start. But she was not long past Ireland before passengers were begging her captain to turn back. As she neared America, the story goes that cargo, one of her masts, most of her furniture and even passengers' children's toys were thrown into the furnaces to keep her boilers going.

Aboard *Great Western* everything proceeded much more smoothly, although passengers would later complain about the smoke and smuts getting everywhere, not to mention the all-pervading smell of the animal fats used to grease her machinery.

Sirius reached New York half a day ahead of *Great Western*, but with hardly any coal left. As a final humiliation, she got stuck on a sandbank at the harbour entrance. A few hours later, *Great Western* swept past with more than 200 tons of unused coal in her bunkers.

Great Western's arrival was a sensation. Thousands turned out to see the magnificent ship coming in. An American newspaper reporter wrote:

Below, on the broad blue water, appeared this huge thing of life, with four masts and emitting volumes of smoke. She looked black and blackguard – rakish, cool, reckless, fierce and forbidding in sombre colours to an extreme. As she neared the Sirius she slackened her movements and took a sweep round, forming a sort of half-circle … After making another turn towards Staten Island, she made another sweep, and shot towards the East River at extraordinary speed. The vast multitude rent the air with their shouts again, waving handkerchiefs, hats, hurrahing![29]

Great Western had proved that safe and quite comfortable steam travel to and from the US was possible. As a result, it was decided to commission a sister ship, an improved version of *Great Western* to be named *Great Britain*. The intention was that the two would operate in tandem, plying a continuous (and profitable) service between Britain and America. Success could be almost guaranteed if the Great Western Steamship Co. were additionally to secure the government contract for carrying mail.

Now restored and preserved in the Bristol dock she was built in, *Great Britain* is acclaimed as a hugely important landmark in maritime history. The first ocean-going ship in the world with both an iron hull and screw propeller, she was also notably larger than any ship ever built. The experience for the Great Western Steamship Co., however, was far from positive. Rising costs, delays and constant revisions to the design meant *Great Britain* was not launched until July 1843, and could not leave Bristol until December 1844 because the entrance locks to Bristol's floating harbour were too small. Once she had left, she would never return to Bristol again under her own power.

Great Britain was the result of Brunel's drive for perfection, regardless of cost, combined with a surge in technological change. The first major modifications to the original plans came about when Brunel, Patterson and Claxton became enthusiastic converts to the idea of an iron hull. Brunel felt less inhibited about designing the hull, given the familiar new building material, and he approached the structure in the same way he would a bridge, designing something which was, first and foremost, immensely strong.

The other radical innovation, the screw propeller, was the aspect that took up most of Brunel's time. Up until then most steamships had been driven through the water by paddles on the sides of the vessel. The problem with paddles is that most of their motion is wasted. The screw propeller was much more efficient. Its inventor was a farmer from Hendon named Francis Pettit Smith. He had used the screw to drive his boat *Archimedes*, then sent it on a promotional tour of British ports. When Brunel saw *Archimedes* in Bristol in 1840 he was instantly captivated. Despite the urgency of building another ship – the mail contract had already gone to Cunard, operating out of Liverpool – he determined that *Great Britain* should be driven by a screw propeller. The resultant trials, errors and design changes proved time consuming and ended up setting back the launch date by years, with damaging financial consequences.

Great Britain eventually made her maiden voyage to New York from Liverpool in July 1845. There were a number of early problems with the propeller breaking. She then accidentally ran aground at Dundrum in Northern Ireland. Her massively strong iron hull survived the beaching – though it was possibly responsible for making compass readings unreliable in the first place. But the company was ruined and the ship was eventually sold at a knockdown price of £25,000.

7

Railway Triumphs, Railway Failures

'He fancied that no-one could do anything but himself.'

Brunel's first two ships were important projects that attracted a lot of attention. Queen Victoria's husband, Prince Albert, came to Bristol – by GWR train of course – to launch *Great Britain.*

Ships, however, accounted for a comparatively small amount of Brunel's time and energy. The great bulk of his career was involved in building railways and the structures associated with them; none more so than the GWR.

Within a few weeks of *Great Western*'s triumphant maiden voyage, Brunel was sufficiently recovered from his accident to attend the opening of the first part of the GWR. On 31 May 1838, 300 guests, including his wife and parents, gathered at Paddington's temporary station and boarded two trains which took them to Maidenhead. It took forty-nine minutes to make the journey, averaging nearly 50mph.

At Maidenhead there was a marquee where the guests had lunch and toasted the success of the GWR. Legend has it Thomas Guppy was so exuberant that on the return journey to London he walked along the carriage roofs while the train was travelling at 40mph. True or not, the tale illustrates a key characteristic of Brunel's GWR. If Guppy really did drunkenly stagger along the carriage roofs, his survival was down not only to luck, but also to the fact that early GWR carriages were wider (and the roofs flatter) than their modern counterparts.

George Stephenson's first trains, as with the majority of the world's trains to this day, travelled on the so-called 'standard gauge', on rails 4ft 8½in apart. This gauge originated in the width of wagon-ways at the mines of north-east England where Stephenson began his career.

To Brunel, the 'Stephenson gauge' was not rational. A wider gauge, he said, would allow for bigger, more powerful locomotives, and thus faster trains. It would also lower the centre of gravity of the rolling stock, making it more stable. GWR was built to Brunel's 'broad gauge' of 7ft, or 7ft ¼in on sharper curves.

Other rail companies would not follow Brunel's lead; everywhere else they were building to the standard. For decades to come the 'break of gauge' at Gloucester, where a GWR line met the standard gauge of the Birmingham and Gloucester Railway, obliging passengers and freight to change trains, was both an irritation and a standing joke.

The gauge question would dominate Brunel's subsequent railway career. The GWR directors together with various engineers and scientists questioned its validity. At one stage the dispute about the gauge and spiralling costs led to an attempt by a faction of Liverpool-based shareholders to oust Brunel as the company's chief engineer. He survived, and the gauge question was temporarily shelved. GWR, he contended, would be a self-contained system which did not have to be compatible with other railways in the country. Hardly anyone else agreed. With the Gauge Act of 1846, the government ordered that henceforth all new passenger-carrying railways should be built to the standard gauge.

Locomotives posed another early challenge for GWR. Brunel turned out to be a poor mechanical engineer. He had, naturally, insisted on writing the specifications for the engines himself, with large driving wheels. When the first were delivered in 1838, however, they turned out to be underpowered, because Brunel had made the boilers too small. The engines were also unreliable.

He was not pleased when the company directors appointed 21-year-old Daniel Gooch as GWR's first Superintendent of Locomotive Engines, as it appeared to undermine his authority. It was, however, an inspired choice. Gooch succeeded in getting most of Brunel's motley collection of locomotives to function adequately before going on to design superb engines of his own.

The first GWR locomotives were manufactured by contractors working to his specifications. It was decided that the company should have a site where locomotives and rolling stock could be repaired and, eventually, built. The result was the giant GWR works at Swindon. A famous Brunel yarn has it that he and Gooch were snatching a picnic lunch beside the line and discussing precisely where the works should be. Brunel threw a sandwich in the air declaring they would be built wherever it landed. In truth, it was Gooch who identified the site in 1840; it was where the gradient became steeper and so thus a good place for more powerful engines. Swindon was also close to a canal which could bring in coal in quantity and there was also a connection to another rail line into the midlands. A whole town grew rapidly around the works, and the first complete locomotives to be built there were in service six years later.

The combination of broad gauge and Gooch's pioneering designs meant that by the late 1840s GWR was running the fastest trains in the world. Together they formed a brilliant Roundhead-and-Cavalier partnership. The dour, taciturn, practical-minded northerner perfectly complemented the flamboyant Brunel. Gooch was, however, often frustrated by Brunel's notorious inability to delegate. 'One feature of Brunel's character,' he later wrote, 'and it was one that gave him a great deal of extra and unnecessary work, was that he fancied no-one could do anything but himself.'[30] When the Prince Consort travelled to Bristol to launch *Great Britain* in 1843, the Gooch-designed 'Firefly' locomotive pulling his train was personally driven by Brunel and Gooch.

The line from London to Bristol had been completed by 1841. The early 1840s also saw the completion of his station at Temple Meads. Designed in partnership with Bristol architect R.S. Pope, research suggests that much of it was Brunel's work. It was the first railway terminus to integrate train shed, offices and passenger facilities. To the Victorians, railways represented the last word in modernity, but its elaborate style, borrowing from Tudor and Jacobean buildings, tried to connect it to earlier eras and project the idea that the railway, a new technology that was dramatically changing Britain in so many ways, was also part of a deeper national tradition.

Brunel was aware of trends and fashions in design and how contradictory they could be. The architect Augustus Pugin (who designed the Houses of Parliament) said that railway stations should look like medieval cathedrals in the Gothic style. Brunel was half in agreement. His station building in Bristol still exists, next to the working station.

One of Brunel's other buildings, and one which is much less acclaimed, was the Royal Western Hotel, nowadays known as Brunel House. This was built in the late 1830s, close to Bristol's docks, and was one of the earliest hotels in Britain specifically designed as such. Unlike the station, it looks much more like an early Victorian gentleman's idea of a country mansion, four storeys high and in Greek revival style, complete with an Ionic colonnade at the front. This was where well-heeled passengers bound for America would stay while awaiting *Great Western*. Again it was designed by Pope, but with directions from Brunel. The building is currently used for offices by Bristol City Council.

At Paddington a temporary station was replaced by a permanent structure in the 1850s. Brunel worked closely with the architect, as usual – in this case Matthew Digby Wyatt. This vast shed of wrought iron and glass was partly inspired by the Crystal Palace built for the Great Exhibition of 1851, a building Brunel greatly admired. When Paddington opened it was the largest train shed in the world (though it featured relatively few decorative flourishes due to the tightening purse strings of the GWR board).

Britain's railways had grown hugely since the first days of the GWR, and had gone through a number of phases of boom and bust. Though operated by a patchwork of private companies, the country now had something approaching a national rail network.

The first major spin-off from GWR was the Bristol & Exeter Railway Company, running from Temple Meads to Exeter. It secured the necessary parliamentary authorisation just a year after the Great Western Railway Act of 1835. Brunel supervised the building of this line. Soon he would also be building lines to Gloucester, Cheltenham and into South Wales.

The Bristol & Exeter was built in stages. The stretch from Bristol to Bridgwater was open by 1841, and that from Bridgwater to Taunton the following year. The line as far as Exeter was completed by 1844. The decision was then taken to extend it to Plymouth and the South Devon Railway Company was formed for that purpose. It would prove to be one of the greatest commercial and technical failures of Brunel's career.

No scientifically minded Victorian seriously believed that steam locomotion was the pinnacle of technology. Steam engines were noisy and dirty, and they consumed large quantities of expensive fuel. A cheaper alternative was highly desirable. Brunel had already spent ten years experimenting with his failed gaz engine, and the South Devon Railway (SDR) offered an opportunity to experiment with another technology. It was still based on steam power, but the hope was that it might prove more efficient. He proposed that part of SDR should be an 'atmospheric railway' using air pressure ('atmosphere') to provide the power.

A small atmospheric railway had already been built, at Dalkey, south of Dublin. Between the rails was a pneumatic tube. Running along this tube was a piston that connected to the train via a slot running along the top. This slot had to be sealed immediately in front of, and behind, the rod connecting piston and train. Air was then pumped out of the tube in front of the piston, while air was allowed in immediately behind it. The resulting vacuum moved the piston along, and the train with it.

Brunel travelled to Dalkey to see the railway in action. Daniel Gooch advised strongly that regular steam locomotives would be cheaper, but Brunel persisted, claiming the new system would be better able to handle some of the steep gradients on the projected line to Plymouth.

A 20-mile stretch between Exeter and Newton Abbot was built as atmospheric railway, with engine houses every 2 or 3 miles to pump the air from the pipe. Brunel designed these in an Italianate style, perhaps thinking it appropriate for the sunny south coast. The best survivor of the system is the station at Starcross, nowadays home to the local boating and fishing club.

From the outset the project was plagued with problems and cost overruns. Brunel started laying a pipe 13in in diameter in 1845, but discovered this would not be adequate. So this had to be pulled up and replaced with a new 15in pipe. The system began operation in September 1847, but was closed after just a year. The pumps had to work more than expected and it was estimated that the cost of moving trains along the line was more than twice that of using ordinary locomotives. What became known as Brunel's 'atmospheric caper' was an expensive failure.

There were also huge technical problems. The slot along the top of the pipes was sealed with leather flaps to maintain the vacuum inside. Since much of the line ran right next to the sea, the leather fell victim to salt spray. The leather had to be greased with tallow to keep it supple and, according to an unsubstantiated legend, the local rats found this delicious.

8

The Later Years

'Brunel's absurd big ship.'

Brunel, like many of the other early engineers, was addicted to work. One could speculate that this was a result of financial insecurity, or perhaps status anxiety. A simpler explanation would be that he did not find any other activity nearly as interesting or gratifying.

He spent weeks at a time away from home, slept less than he should have and chain-smoked cigars. His responsibilities were immense: from the 1830s onwards he was working for several clients at any one time, almost always on railway projects. There were still relatively few railway engineers of proven talent on the ground and his reputation was considerable – offers of employment came flooding in, not just to work in Britain and Ireland, but also, from the 1840s, on railways in Italy, India and Australia too.

Railways were a British invention and British railway engineers enjoyed a near-monopoly of expertise worldwide for some years. If a government or private company in another country wanted a railway, then they needed a British engineer. Brunel was so busy in the UK that he took on comparatively few projects abroad. He never travelled to India or Australia, though he did make two brief visits to Italy in the 1840s for railway projects in Piedmont and Tuscany. For the most part he supervised overseas rail schemes by correspondence, with the work on the spot overseen by local or British engineers acting on his orders.

The workload took its toll, as did the various falls and scrapes Brunel suffered during his career. Apart from his injuries in the Thames Tunnel and on *Great Western*, he endured several lesser mishaps. As a keen rider, he often fell or got thrown from horses and his disregard for physical danger does not seem to have diminished as he got older. In July 1851 he even played a general in the so-called 'Battle of Mickleton Tunnel'. This was the result of yet another dispute with a contractor who was owed money. Brunel led a force of navvies in a bid to retake control of a stretch of the Oxford, Worcester & Wolverhampton Railway, one of his many minor clients. The contractor, Robert Mudge-Marchant, refused to relinquish possession of the site to a new contractor and used his own navvies to guard it. This episode, which may have involved as many as 3,000 men, is sometimes grandly written up as the last battle on English soil between two private armies, though to contemporaries it looked more like an old-fashioned brawl, albeit one in which the local magistrates, supported by police constables armed with cutlasses as well as members of the Gloucestershire artillery, tried to keep the peace. There were several cracked skulls and broken bones, but no fatalities. The presence of Brunel and his men made it impossible for Mudge-Marchant to continue work and both parties agreed terms just as the authorities summoned extra troops to the scene.

By this time he was also thinking of building another ship. Like its two predecessors, it would be the biggest ever undertaken. His ambitions this time were on a truly gargantuan scale. *Great Eastern*, when her plans were finalised, would be 690ft long, more than twice the length of any other ship in existence. At 22,500 tons, this leviathan would be six times the size of any ship ever built. The rest of the numbers were equally staggering: she would carry 18,000 tons of coal and cargo, as well as 4,000 passengers or, at a push, 10,000 soldiers. She would be driven by both a screw propeller and by paddles, but would also save on her immense fuel bill with six masts carrying 65,000sq. yd of sail. Her two engines – one of 1,000hp for paddles and one of 1,600hp for the screw – would be run by seventy-two furnaces belching smoke from six funnels.

'Everybody understands the "proposed large steamer" to mean "Brunel's absurd big ship",' he wrote sardonically to a friend.[31]

Except that it wasn't entirely Brunel's ship. This time he was working with John Scott Russell (1808–82), a brilliant Scottish engineer and pioneer of new hull designs. Russell had been running a shipyard on the Thames since 1847 and was one of the founders of the Royal Society of Arts, as well as being one of the first organisers of the Great Exhibition of 1851. Russell was as stubborn and sure of himself as Brunel. Both men moved in a comparatively small, elite circle of engineers and scientists. Brunel had consulted Russell on the design for the hull of *Great Britain* and they now formed a partnership for the *Great Eastern* project.

The central idea was to build a ship that could undertake very long voyages – to America and India, for example – and return again without having to refuel. As ever-increasing numbers of ocean-going vessels, especially those carrying passengers, were running under steam power, the problem was refuelling. Coal had to be shipped from Britain to various points around the world, but this was expensive. Refuelling in some foreign land or outpost of empire could cost five times as much as taking on coal in Britain. *Great Eastern*'s unique selling point was its economy of scale.

As usual, a new company was formed to build and run her, but the 'absurd big ship' was a hard proposition to sell to investors. The initial concept was sketched out in 1851, but it would be another three years before construction could begin at Russell's yard in Millwall. Workers and sailors alike came to regard the ship as cursed. Brunel and Russell fell out, and for much of the time they were barely on speaking terms. In among all the money problems, there was a strong suspicion that Russell had taken 900 tons of iron meant for *Great Eastern* to use in his other projects. The two also fell out over a newspaper report which suggested that the ship was Russell's idea, prompting Brunel to think Russell was conspiring against him.

Great Eastern was finally ready for launch in 1857. Because of her massive length, it had been decided that she should be launched sideways into the river; the traditional stern-first method would have seen her run aground on the opposite bank. Brunel insisted, however, that she be launched along iron rails rather than the usual greased wooden slipway. After three months, and an expenditure of £120,000 that should have been spent on fitting her out, the ship was finally floated. But the company sank – *Great Eastern* lay idle for almost a year while her backers tried to form a new firm to finish her.

The five years of stress involved in building *Great Eastern* must have taken its toll on Brunel's health. As he entered his fifties he was, by the standards of the time, quite old. All the accidents he had endured down the years started to weigh on him, as, no doubt, did all the nights with little or no sleep, not to mention his addiction to tobacco. Accounts of him from this time tell of his shortening temper, and the decline of the physical and mental faculties which had enabled him to juggle so many different jobs at the same time at the height of his career.

If the stresses and tolls of a busy life had been all that Brunel had to contend with, then perhaps he could have taken the quiet advice offered by friends, eased up on his workload and perhaps focused on the home he hoped to build in Devon. In the spring of 1858 he allowed himself to be persuaded to take a holiday with Mary in France – they took the waters at Vichy – and then Switzerland before returning via Holland. But the break did him little good. He recognised that he had a problem, writing: 'I would not trouble you with an invalid's journal … being weak, I am regularly floored with a concatenation of evils.'[32]

Accounts of Brunel's later years tend to be dominated by the difficulties surrounding *Great Eastern*, but this period also saw at least two unquestionable triumphs. The first was a prefabricated hospital.

In 1855 Britain was at war with Russia in the Crimea. Brunel was approached by his old friend and brother-in-law, Benjamin Hawes, who was undersecretary at the War Office. He explained that the government urgently needed a hospital to be built in the Crimea. Brunel designed a complex of prefabricated wooden buildings which could be shipped out and erected at a suitable site near the army's hospital at Scutari (Üsküdar) in Turkey, where Florence Nightingale was working.

The wood and canvas buildings were produced and shipped, like an immense piece of flatpack furniture, within five months, most of the work being done by the Gloucester firm of William Eassie, which had made prefabricated wooden huts for gold prospectors in Australia and was also supplying wooden facilities for *Great Eastern*. Although the units arrived as the Crimean War was reaching a close, they were a great and instant success. The design incorporated sanitation, drainage and ventilation, and the chances of patients surviving here were said to be significantly better than those at the main Scutari hospital. Florence Nightingale called them 'those magnificent huts'.

Brunel's second triumph during this period was another bridge. The railway from south Devon was being extended from Plymouth all the way to Falmouth in Cornwall. The River Tamar, over which the line would have to cross near Plymouth, was a formidable obstacle. At first, a train ferry was proposed, but the government refused permission. Brunel had been engaged to come up with a solution in the mid-1840s, but the Admiralty turned down his initial plan for a timber viaduct because any bridge had to be high enough for vessels from the Royal Navy's Plymouth base to pass beneath.

Brunel proposed a bridge at Saltash, heavily influenced by Robert Stephenson's Britannia Bridge across the Menai Strait to Anglesey. It would consist of two long iron 'lenticular trusses' a hundred feet above the water, with a wrought-iron tubular arch at the top and a pair of chains at the bottom. Both would connect to a central pier in mid-river, in effect creating a pair of suspension bridges.

The construction was complex and hazardous. Work began in 1854 after several surveys of the riverbed had been carried out to choose the best location. For the central pier, an immense cylinder was lowered vertically into the Tamar. Inside this was a diving bell in which workers had to remove sand, silt, mud and oyster shells before they could build firm foundations on rock. Once this was built, the 1,000-ton trusses had to be lifted into place. Brunel had been present to advise when Robert Stephenson had carried out a similar operation with the huge rectangular iron tubes on his Britannia Bridge. Stephenson returned the favour on 1 September 1857, when Brunel personally supervised the manoeuvring of the first truss into position. It was floated out into the river on pontoons and, as thousands of sightseers looked on, he co-ordinated the army of workmen moving it into position, using flag signals, as one witness put it, like a conductor with an orchestra. The trusses would be jacked up slowly into position over the coming months as the piers were built beneath them.

The Royal Albert Bridge, as it was called, was formally opened by Prince Albert on 2 May 1859. Vast crowds turned out to see the Prince Consort's arrival (enterprising local farmers actually charged spectators to enter fields next to the bridge) and, after the usual speeches, watch him travel by train across the bridge. The journey was a very slow one so that all the details of the bridge's construction could be explained to His Royal Highness, who took a passionate interest in new technology. *The Times* commented:

> Its height from the water is about 120 feet, and so slight looks the web of neatly arranged beams, which, rising one upon another, carry the roadway high over all, that it taxes the passenger's confidence in Mr. Brunel to the very utmost to venture on it in a heavy train. It has, of course, been properly tested …[33]

Brunel was not present at the ceremony. His health had not improved. Sir Benjamin Brodie, one of the leading physicians of the day, had referred him to Dr Bright, who confirmed that Brunel was suffering from Bright's Disease, nowadays known as nephritis, a kidney inflammation that can have a wide range of symptoms. On his doctors' orders he took another vacation, this time in Egypt, accompanied by Mary, his son Henry and a physician. The story goes that during a rough passage by paddle steamer across the Mediterranean, everyone was so seasick that all retired to their cabins apart from Brunel, who was so preoccupied with measuring the ship's pitching and rolling, and observing the wind and the action of the paddles that he failed to realise everyone else had gone.

In Egypt the Brunels visited ancient ruins on donkeys and shot at bottles in the Nile from the rails of the steamer taking them up river. They spent Christmas Day in Cairo with Robert Stephenson, who was also ill. It would be the last time the two men met.

The Brunels came home via Rome, but the holiday proved of limited benefit. Over the coming months he spent much of his time in bed.

After its problematic start the *Great Eastern* project seemed to be going well. Her engines, decorations and furniture having been fitted, she was due to make her first voyage, from London to Weymouth and Holyhead, on 3 September 1859. Brunel went aboard the day before to inspect the engines. At about midday he posed for a photograph near one of the funnels, looking thin and frail and leaning on a stick. Shortly afterwards he had a stroke – a common enough consequence of nephritis – and was taken home, paralysed but conscious.

Anxiously awaiting news of the ship on his sickbed, he was told on 10 September that there had been an explosion aboard two days previously. The cause was trivial and the damage slight, but five men had been killed and many more injured.

On the afternoon of Thursday 15 September he spoke to each member of his family in turn. That evening he died peacefully in his sleep.

Brunel's death was headline news, covered in a way that nowadays would only be matched by the passing of a major celebrity. The *Illustrated London News* led on its front page with an atrocious portrait of him surrounded by smaller pictures of his ships and some of the bridges. *The Times* obituary was long and typically Victorian in its fulsome praise for a man who laboured on through illness and pain: 'Possessing a mind strong in the consciousness of rectitude, he pursued, in single hearted truthfulness, what he believed to be the course of duty.'[34] Back in Bristol an anonymous hack writer on one of the local papers summoned up all his lyrical powers to write of a man who had 'by enabling us to triumph over the forces of this material world, conferred benefits upon the human race which will endure and fructify even after the great monuments he himself has erected to his genius shall have crumbled into dust'.[35]

Not long afterwards, Brunel's friend Robert Stephenson died and was buried at Westminster Abbey, where all the greatest national heroes and heroines are laid to rest. No such honour was offered to Brunel; celebrity he may have been, but he was a much more divisive figure than Stephenson. Instead, he was buried at Kensal Green Cemetery in west London, joining his mother and father in the family vault. His father had, in fact, had a small hand in designing Kensal Green, one of the capital's great Victorian cemeteries – a vast necropolis built to accommodate the huge numbers of bodies thrown up by the growing population of the living. In that sense, Brunel's burial was every bit as 'modern' as his life had been.

The funeral was meant to be a small family affair. Status-conscious Victorians tended to measure the social cachet of a funeral by the number of carriages in attendance. In Brunel's case there were only two for family members and twelve others, making it relatively modest. For all that, hundreds of people, many of them rail workers, lined the route and all the shops in Duke Street closed as a mark of respect. At the cemetery, a large number of gentlemen of the Society of Civil Engineers followed the procession to the grave.

After hearing of Brunel's passing, Daniel Gooch wrote:

> By his death the greatest of England's engineers was lost, the man with the greatest originality of thought and power of execution, bold in his plans but right. The commercial world thought him extravagant; but although he was so, great things are not done by those who sit down and count the cost of every thought and act. He was a true and sincere friend, a man of the highest honour, and his loss was deeply deplored by all who had the pleasure to know him.[36]

9

Legacies

'Bold in his plans, but right.'

Just before dawn on Saturday 21 May 1892, managers and foremen moved through stations and engine sheds along the GWR line from Paddington to Penzance rousing sleeping men. In remote spots, the bosses marched around temporary camps where workers slept in large tents.

Within minutes, an army of almost 5,000 was stirring, yawning, picking up tools and mustering along 170 miles of track. There was a hard day ahead. Some were GWR employees, but most were temporary staff who had been told they would be working for as long as the light lasted, and that they would be up again at dawn the following day.

Organised in teams of twenty, they set to work moving and tying in rails, laying new points and crossings. Meanwhile, GWR staff shunted redundant locomotives and rolling stock to a vast complex at Swindon, laying up engines, wagons and carriages along 15 miles of specially prepared sidings.

A few hours later, the nation's more affluent citizens sat down to breakfast and read in their morning papers how the very last broad gauge trains had left the night before. At Dawlish station, the final two passenger trains stopped alongside one another, headed in opposite directions. People opened their carriage windows to shake hands with one another. The papers reported that everyone sang *Auld Land Syne.*

The workmen continued their labours throughout the day, stopping only briefly to eat. They had been told to bring their own provisions, and the company had also laid on 5 tons of oatmeal, which they consumed as thin gruel. Many smoked pipes as they worked and each man had been given 2oz of tobacco, free of charge, by W.D. and H.O. Wills of Bristol. Alcohol was forbidden on pain of instant dismissal.

Everything for the end of the broad gauge had been planned in meticulous detail. Managers along the line scurried about, giving orders, making decisions and trying to solve problems, working from a specially printed manual which ran to eighty pages. By the following afternoon, the last vestiges of the broad gauge had disappeared forever from the GWR. From now on, it was entirely standard gauge.

The GWR had long since acquired control of the South Devon and Cornwall rail companies, and had for years been gradually converting its entire system to standard gauge. The line from Paddington as far as Exeter had been 'double gauged' – lines were of three rails instead of two – accommodating trains of both types. It was still entirely broad gauge west of Exeter, though. This was all changed in the space of thirty-one hours, and the whole system was operating smoothly and to timetable by Monday.

By now, railways had lost their novelty, and they were not always regarded with affection. For instance, the

Somerset and Dorset (S&D) was nicknamed the 'Slow and Dirty', while the Oxford, Worcester and Wolverhampton (OW&W) was the 'Old Worse and Worse'. But not the GWR: the GWR was always 'God's Wonderful Railway'.

That was Brunel's legacy. He had created a railway running on a gauge system incompatible with the other railways it connected to, but he had also bequeathed a company that could smoothly and efficiently implement a complete change of gauge in the space of a single weekend.

The GWR and the structures associated with it are the greatest tangible assets that Brunel left to modern Britain. His other grand projects had more mixed fortunes. Nobody ever tried to build an atmospheric railway again and the gaz engine lives on only as a footnote in engineering history, waiting to be picked up by some steampunk novelist or filmmaker.

Great Western plied her profitable way between Britain and America for some years before being sold when the company's losses on *Great Britain* became unsustainable. She then ran between Britain and the West Indies for a long time, and was used as a troopship for the Crimean War. She was broken up in 1856, a few years before Brunel died.

Great Eastern, having ruined the Eastern Steam Navigation Company financially, was sold for a fraction of the sum she had cost to build. She found a useful role for a while in the 1860s when Daniel Gooch, by then chief engineer of the Telegraph Construction & Maintenance Company, used her to lay 2,600 miles of telegraph cable under the Atlantic. (She was the only ship big enough to carry all the cabling.) As a result of her contribution, for the first time in history people in Britain and America could communicate almost instantly.

The rest of *Great Eastern*'s career was not so happy. After periods as a liner, floating concert hall and even advertising hoarding, she was sold and broken up on Merseyside in 1889–90. It took almost two years to take her apart, and yet another Brunel yarn was generated. The story this time (for which there is no evidence) was that the skeletons of a man and boy – a riveter and his young assistant – were found in the space between the inner and outer hulls. This was taken as further evidence that *Great Eastern* had been jinxed. One of the few remnants nowadays is a flagpole made from one of her masts at Liverpool FC's Anfield ground.

In 1860, John Hawkshaw, president of the Institution of Civil Engineers, and his fellow engineer William Barlow, suggested that the chains from the Hungerford suspension bridge in London, which was about to be replaced, could be used to complete the bridge in Clifton. The Hungerford pedestrian bridge had been one of Brunel's minor projects in the 1840s and had, by a nice twist of irony, used the chains Brunel commissioned for the postponed Clifton bridge. Hawkshaw and Barlow felt the uncompleted bridge was an embarrassment to their profession, and they wanted to finish the job as a monument to Brunel. A new company was formed, money was raised, and the Hungerford chains were purchased and taken to Bristol on the GWR.

Hawkshaw and Barlow made many changes to Brunel's design. A third chain was added to the two he specified, in order to support additional weight. There were new anchorage pits and significantly more ironwork. The Egyptian decorations were never added, nor were the cast-iron panels showing how the bridge had been made.

It has been argued that the Clifton Suspension Bridge, which opened to great fanfare in 1864 (crowds, military bands, speeches, a parade of Bristol's different professions all on the front cover of the *Illustrated London News*), is not really Brunel's design. His own family obviously felt so and turned down their invitation to the opening. In all its essentials, however, the bridge is more Brunel's than anyone else's. The way Hawkshaw and Barlow strengthened it did both the bridge and Brunel's memory a great service. The original design was for a structure that would take pedestrians and a few horses, carts and carriages. The bridge that actually got built regularly copes with 10,000 vehicles daily and everyone knows it as Brunel's work.

Great Britain had a long and adventurous career before ending up in the Falkland Islands in the 1880s. Following storm damage she was judged unseaworthy and for many decades was used as a floating warehouse before being towed ashore and abandoned. She performed one last service to her country in 1939. Following the Battle of the River Plate between Royal Navy ships and the German battleship *Graf Spee*, some of her ironwork was cannibalised to help patch up HMS *Exeter*.

In 1967, the naval architect Ewan Corlett wrote a letter to *The Times*:

Sir, – The first iron built ocean-going steamship and the first such ship to be driven entirely by a propeller was the Great Britain, designed and launched by Isambard Kingdom Brunel. This, the forefather of all modern ships, is lying a beached hulk in the Falkland islands at this moment.

The Cutty Sark has rightly been preserved at Greenwich and H.M.S. Victory at Portsmouth. Historically the Great Britain has an equal claim to fame and yet nothing has been done to document her hulk, let alone recover it and preserve it for the record.[37]

This letter set in motion a thrilling adventure worthy of Brunel himself. A completely unseaworthy 3,000-ton wreck was brought home across 7,500 nautical miles of some of the most hostile seas on earth.

Funded by a patriotic millionaire, Sir Jack ('Union Jack') Hayward, the salvage operation got under way in the spring of 1970. The ship was put onto a special pontoon. A huge crack on one side of the hull was bunged up with mattresses donated by Falkland Islanders.

The pontoon was towed back through the South and North Atlantic to the Bristol Channel by tug. On 5 July 1970, having been taken off the pontoon, she was pulled up the Avon and home to Bristol, watched by over 100,000 sightseers and 8 million television viewers. On 19 July she was finally returned to the dock where she had been built. More than four decades on, painstakingly restored, she is now an award-winning visitor attraction.

The idea that Brunel 'built the modern world' is absurd, yet he certainly played a leading role in its creation. The changes that Britain saw between 1800 and 1900 were even more profound than those between 1900 and 2000.

When Brunel was born, most Britons lived their whole lives within a few miles of their birthplace. Few ever dreamed of migrating to another town, let alone another country, and hardly any travelled for pleasure. Journeying any distance that could not be covered on foot was expensive, uncomfortable and often perilous.

The greatest speed at which anyone could travel was restricted to a brief gallop on a thoroughbred horse and the greatest speed at which people could communicate over distance was dictated by the Post Office. Though Britain was the most industrially advanced country in the world, most people still lived in small towns and villages and most depended for their subsistence partly or wholly on working the land. The national diet was overwhelmingly seasonal and local.

By the time Brunel died, a recognisably modern world was taking shape. This new environment was one in which most people bought food from shops or markets in the cities and large towns where most of them now lived, with money paid them as a wage or salary in return for working set hours for a permanent employer. Grocers' shops were filled with foodstuffs from around the country, and even from around the world; indeed, much of Britain's bread, the most basic staple, was now made with imported wheat. Other shops sold consumer goods, mass-produced in mechanised factories dozens and sometimes hundreds of miles away.

Travel, whether as part of the waves of migration around the British Isles or emigration from Britain to Europe, North America and the empire, was affordable and safe. The postal service was cheap, fast and efficient. Businessmen and diplomats routinely communicated using the electric telegraph, and even working people could send telegrams if they needed. As society became more complex, schooling stopped being the preserve of a privileged minority and access to education became universal.

These changes were financed by government, and by confidently aggressive capitalists exploiting new inventions and processes. But ultimately, this new world was the work of engineers.

Brunel's contributions to these changes included the world's first fully integrated railway system, two vessels that changed shipbuilding and steam navigation forever and a third ship which (though he never intended it as such) made transatlantic communication possible.

With each of these, and his other works, there were significant unforeseen, but usually benign, consequences. To take one example: the very last broad gauge train on the GWR was not one whose passengers shook hands at Dawlish. It was a goods train from Penzance carrying 80 tons of fish. By 1892 fish was a regular part of every Briton's diet. Fish were plentiful around the country's coast and there were fleets of boats going out to catch them. This was because the new railways enabled fresh fish to be transported quickly, and in huge quantities, to Britain's towns and cities before it perished. Cheap fish helped feed Britain's urban working class and in turn made possible the growth of city populations. Some people set up in business selling fried fish and when their oil grew too hot they would throw pieces of potato in to cool it a little. Soon their customers were asking for these 'chips' as well.

Brunel was not responsible for fish and chips – but he was one of the key architects of the world that made fish and chips possible, and by extrapolation the modern fast-food industry.

Brunel's physical legacies are there for all to see. Everyone can appreciate the beauty of the things he built, his soaring ambition and the purity and honesty of his intentions. His psychological legacy is less measurable. As an adolescent he had scribbled in his diary about how he wanted to be 'the first Engineer and an example for future ones'. It was a goal he certainly achieved. He continues to inspire present generations of engineers, architects, artists and project managers in a way that few others can. Kenneth Clark's line continues to resonate: Brunel was a visionary, he was 'in love with the impossible'.

There is much in the modern world that Brunel would find fascinating. Powered flight, for instance, and computers of course. There is also much of which he would disapprove: the increased role of government and bureaucracy in all our lives would frustrate him intensely. He would almost certainly love the internet, not just as a technical achievement, but because (for now at least) it is so difficult for governments to control.

Picture him, freshly arrived by time machine, sitting on an uncomfortable green chair before some Parliamentary Select Committee. Someone would remind him that this is a no-smoking area, and after tetchily stubbing out his cigar, he might sardonically offer the view that the much-vaunted HS2 rail line is a waste of time and money. Maybe he would suggest that Britain needs to recapture her primacy in engineering and technology through the application of the latest ideas. Why bother with trains when we can have robotically controlled cars? Why not cut through all the talk and red tape and enable business and academics to turn us into a world leader in green technologies? Should we not be looking at some massive-scale solution to climate change? And shouldn't we be in space, by the way? Getting into his stride, he might rail against the British fear of maths or how society and the education system separate the arts and sciences where they should be intimately intertwined.

While stuck in his hotel room he would probably read as much as he could (he wouldn't watch documentaries – too inefficient a way of absorbing information) about the Apollo space programme, a project born of a soaring ambition with the seemingly impossible goal of putting a man on the moon. And after Apollo? Perhaps at this point he would ask to go back to his own time. Though he might take a list of derby winners with him, not to make money you understand, but as a giant joke to impress his friends.

Notes

1   Latimer, J., *The Annals of Bristol in the Nineteenth Century* (W.F. Morgan, 1887), p. 191.

2   Ibid., p. 219.

3   'Nominate England's greatest icon', 8 June 2004, www.bbc.co.uk.

4   *Western Daily Press*, 23 May 1892.

5   Clark, K., *Civilisation* (BBC & John Murray, 1969), p. 331.

6   Quoted in Fox, S., *The Ocean Railway* (Harper Perennial, 2004), p. 65.

7   Smiles, S., *Industrial Biography: Iron Workers and Tool Makers* (John Murray, 1863), p. 215.

8   Ibid., p. 217.

9   Quoted in Vaughan, A., *Isambard Kingdom Brunel: Engineering Knight-Errant* (John Murray, 2003), p. 7.

10 Brunel, I., *The Life of Isambard Kingdom Brunel, Civil Engineer* (Longmans, Green & Co., 1870), p. 5.

11 'The Personal Journal of I.K. Brunel' (University of Bristol Special Collections, DM 1306/ll).

12 Quoted in Rolt, L.T.C., *Isambard Kingdom Brunel* (Penguin Books, 1985 edn), p. 82.

13 Ibid., p. 85.

14   *Bristol Mercury*, 21 June 1831.

15   *The Life of Isambard Kingdom Brunel, Civil
      Engineer*, op. cit., p. 78.

16   *The Annals of Bristol in the Nineteenth Century*, op.
      cit., p. 133.

17   Quoted in Kelly, A. & M., *Brunel: In Love with
      the Impossible* (Bristol Cultural Development
      Partnership, 2006), p. 136.

18   *The Life of Isambard Kingdom Brunel, Civil
      Engineer*, op. cit., p. 76.

19   Ibid., p. 97.

20   Ibid., p. 70.

21   *Brunel: In Love with the Impossible*, op. cit., p. 239.

22   'A Civil Engineer', in *Personal Recollections of
      English Engineers, and of the Introduction of the
      Railway System into the United Kingdom* (Hodder
      & Stoughton, 1868), p. 405.

23   *The Life of Isambard Kingdom Brunel, Civil
      Engineer*, op. cit., p. 75.

24   Quoted in Fox, S., *The Ocean Railway: Isambard
      Kingdom Brunel, Samuel Cunard and the
      Revolutionary World of the Great Atlantic
      Steamships* (HarperCollins, 2003), p. 63.

25   'The Personal journal of I.K. Brunel', op. cit.

26   *Isambard Kingdom Brunel*, op. cit., p. 120.

27   Quoted in ibid., p. 134.

28   Quoted in *Isambard Kingdom Brunel: Engineering
      Knight-Errant*, op. cit., p. 200.

29   *Isambard Kingdom Brunel*, op. cit., p. 259.

30   *Isambard Kingdom Brunel: Engineering Knight-Errant*, op. cit., p. 82.

31   Pugsley, A., *The Works of Isambard Kingdom Brunel: An Engineering Appreciation* (Bristol University/ The Institution of Civil Engineers, 1976), p. 20.

32   *Isambard Kingdom Brunel*, op. cit., p. 369.

33   *The Times*, 4 May 1859.

34   *The Times*, 19 September 1859.

35   *Western Daily Press*, 19 September 1859.

36   Gooch, D., *Diaries of Sir Daniel Gooch, Baronet* (K. Paul, Trench Trübner & Co. Ltd, 1892), p. 70.

37   *The Times*, 11 November 1967.

Timeline

1806	9 April: Born Portsea, Portsmouth
1808	Family moves to London
1814	Goes to Dr Morrell's school, Hove
1815	Napoleonic Wars end with defeat of Napoleon at Waterloo
1820	Goes to Caen College, Normandy, then Lycée Henri-Quatre, Paris
1821	Marc Brunel imprisoned for debt for three months
1822	Studies under clockmaker Abraham-Louis Bréguet for a year
1825	Marc Brunel begins work on Thames tunnel
1827	Marc puts Isambard in charge of Thames tunnel project
1828	Injured in accident in Thames tunnel
1830	Elected Fellow of Royal Society
1831	Work begins on Clifton Suspension Bridge Bristol riots
1832	Great Reform Act passed
1833	Slavery abolished in Britain and throughout its empire
Appointed engineer to Great Western Railway

1836	5 July: Marries Mary Elizabeth Horsley (1813–81)
	First instalments of *Pickwick Papers*, Dickens' first novel, published
1837	Death of King William IV, accession of Queen Victoria
	Birth of Isambard, first of three children
1838	Maiden voyage of *Great Western* to New York
	First stretch of Great Western Railway opens, from Paddington to Maidenhead
1840	Construction of Swindon railway works begins
1841	Thames tunnel completed
	Great Western Rail through link from London to Bristol completed
	Marc Brunel knighted
1843	*Great Britain* launched
	Accidentally inhales a coin when performing a conjuring trick
1844	*Great Britain* leaves Bristol
1845	*Great Britain* makes maiden voyage from Liverpool to New York
1846	*Great Britain* runs aground at Dundrum, Co. Down, Ireland
	Parliament passes Gauge Act, making standard gauge compulsory on all new railways
1847	South Devon Railway's atmospheric system begins operation

1848	Atmospheric system abandoned
1849	12 December: Death of Marc Brunel
1853	Outbreak of Crimean War
1854	London Paddington station opened
1855	Designs pre-fabricated hospital for Crimean War
1856	End of Crimean War
1857	Awarded honorary degree by Oxford University
1858	*Great Eastern* launched Takes holiday in Egypt on medical advice, accompanied by Mary and son Henry
1859	Royal Albert Bridge opens 15 September: Dies; buried in family vault at Kensal Green cemetery
1864	Clifton Suspension Bridge opens
1865	*Great Eastern* undertakes first cable-laying voyage
1870	Son Isambard publishes biography of his father
1889	*Great Eastern* scrapped
1892	Last broad gauge track on Great Western Railway removed
1970	*Great Britain* brought home from Falkland Islands
2002	Comes second to Winston Churchill in BBC poll of 'greatest Britons'
2012	Portrayed by Kenneth Branagh in opening ceremony of London Olympics

Further Reading

Brindle, Steven & Cruickshank, Dan, *Brunel: The Man Who Built the World* (Weidenfeld & Nicholson, 2005)

Brunel, Isambard, *The Life of Isambard Kingdom Brunel, Civil Engineer* (Longmans, Green & Co., 1870)

Buchanan, Angus & Williams, Michael, *Brunel's Bristol* (Redcliffe Press, 1982)

Buchanan, Angus, *Brunel: The Life and Times of Isambard Kingdom Brunel* (Hambledon & London, 2002)

Byrne, Eugene & Gurr, Simon, *Isambard Kingdom Brunel: A Graphic Biography* (Bristol Cultural Development Partnership, 2006)

Coleman, Terry, *The Railway Navvies: A History of the Men Who Made the Railways* (Hutchinson, 1965)

Fox, Stephen, *The Ocean Railway: Isambard Kingdom Brunel, Samuel Cunard and the Revolutionary World of the Great Atlantic Steamships* (HarperCollins, 2003)

Kelly, Andrew & Melanie (eds), *Brunel: In Love With the Impossible* (Bristol Cultural Development Partnership, 2006)

Rolt, L.T.C., *Isambard Kingdom Brunel* (Longman, 1957)

Vaughan, Adrian, *Isambard Kingdom Brunel: Engineering Knight-Errant* (John Murray, 1991)

Vaughan, Adrian, *The Intemperate Engineer: Isambard Kingdom Brunel in his own Words* (Ian Allan, 2010)

Wolmar, Christian, *Fire and Steam: How the Railways Transformed Britain* (Atlantic Books, 2008)

Web Links

www.brunel-museum.org.uk – The Brunel Museum
    in Rotherhithe, London, sited directly above the
    Thames Tunnel

www.ssgreatbritain.org – Site of Brunel's SS *Great Britain*
    in Bristol

www.brunel200.com – Website for 200th anniversary of
    Brunel's birth includes a large amount of material

www.bris.ac.uk/library/resources/specialcollections/
    archives/brunel/ – The Brunel Institute, run by
    Bristol University and SS *Great Britain*

www.brunel.ac.uk/about/history/isambard-kingdom-
    brunel – Brunel University's web pages about
    Brunel, including L.T.C. Rolt's 1958 lecture

www.clifton-suspension-bridge.org.uk – Website of the
    Clifton Suspension Bridge, Bristol

www.didcotrailwaycentre.org.uk – The Great Western
    Society's Railway Centre in Oxfordshire

www.greatwestern.org.uk – The Great Western Archive,
    for information on GWR

www.mybrunel.co.uk – General site about life and work
    of Brunel

www.ikbrunel.org.uk – Website aimed mostly at children,
    promoting a children's novel
www.royal-albert-bridge.co.uk – Research information
    on the Royal Albert Bridge at Saltash
www.steam-museum.org.uk – Official website of STEAM,
    the Great Western Railway museum in Swindon
http://archive.org/details/lifeofisambardki00brunuoft –
    Full text of *The Life of Isambard Kingdom Brunel,*
    Civil Engineer by his son Isambard

Giuseppe **Verdi** Henry V **Brunel** Pope John
Paul II **Jane Austen** William the Conqueror
Abraham Lincoln Robert the Bruce **Charles
Darwin** Buddha **Elizabeth I** Horatio Nelson
Wellington Hannibal & Scipio **Jesus** Joan of Arc
Anne Frank Alfred the Great **King Arthur** Henry
Ford **Nelson Mandela**